Pairing STEAM with Stories

ALA Editions purchases fund advocacy, awareness, and accreditation programs for library professionals worldwide.

Elizabeth McChesney and the Chicago Public Library
Brett Nicholas and the Museum of Science and Industry

PAIRING
STEAM

WITH STORIES

46 Hands-On Activities for Children

ALA
Editions
CHICAGO | 2020

Extensive effort has gone into ensuring the reliability of the information in this book; however, the publisher makes no warranty, express or implied, with respect to the material contained herein.

ISBN: 978-0-8389-4749-4 (paper)

Library of Congress Cataloging-in-Publication Data
Names: McChesney, Elizabeth M., author. | Nicholas, Brett, author. | Chicago Public Library, author. | Museum of Science and Industry (Chicago, Ill.), author.
Title: Pairing STEAM with stories : 46 hands-on activities for children / Elizabeth McChesney and the Chicago Public Library, Brett Nicholas and the Museum of Science and Industry.
Description: Chicago : ALA Editions, 2020. | Includes bibliographical references and index. | Summary: "This book provides 46 hands-on STEAM activities that librarians and museum educators can implement"—Provided by publisher.
Identifiers: LCCN 2020006950 | ISBN 9780838947494 (paperback)
Subjects: LCSH: Children's libraries—Activity programs—Case studies. | Children's libraries—Activity programs—Illinois—Chicago. | Libraries and museums—Illinois—Chicago. | Science—Study and teaching (Elementary)—Activity programs. | Technology—Study and teaching (Elementary—Activity programs. | Engineering—Study and teaching (Elementary)—Activity programs. | Mathematics—Study and teaching (Elementary)—Activity programs. | Science and the arts—Study and teaching (Elementary)
Classification: LCC Z718.3 .M34 2020 | DDC 027.62/50977311—dc23
LC record available at https://lccn.loc.gov/2020006950

Design by Alejandra Diaz in the Questa and Dita typefaces.

♾ This paper meets the requirements of ANSI/NISO Z39.48-1992 (Permanence of Paper).
Printed in the United States of America

24 23 22 21 20   5 4 3 2 1

TO ALL THE CHILDREN OF CHICAGO—
especially Arthur, Maren, and Phoebe

CONTENTS

~ Appendixes ~

FOREWORD

In the twenty-first century, educators in and out of school are concerned with the new skills and aptitudes our children need to be successful in a changing, more competitive and connected global community and economy. Summer months have proved to be a powerful time to help kids learn how to make sense of a fast and vastly changing world: empowering and equipping them with the skills, experiences, and resources they need to become resilient lifelong learners who can take control of their future. Helping kids navigate this terrain, develop a growth mind-set, and learn new ways to solve problems and answer questions in an informal education setting like the library is critical to the success of the next generation.

Throughout my career working to close the achievement and opportunity gaps between lower and higher income students, I have seen why and how high-quality summer programs can change lives. Summer learning programs like those run in Chicago provide a unique time and space to be reflective and focus on *improvement* of skills for both children and adult educators.

As the ideas in this book demonstrate, summer also provides a rare and meaningful time to promote *innovation* and experiment with new ideas in education. Many new and successful city-wide initiatives and programs first started out in the summer before they scaled.

Summer is also an opportune time to practice *integration*—to bring many unlikely yet like-minded allies in a community under one big tent to support the well-being of every child during the critical summer months in ways they are too busy to do during the school year. But most important, summer is a powerful time of *impact* on the lives of children. It offers a community a high return on investment when the lessons learned from hands-on experiential opportunities are both immediate and lasting. Studies like *Shaping Summertime Experiences: Opportunities to Promote Healthy Development and Well-Being for Children and Youth*, a 2019 report from the National Academies of Sciences, Engineering, and Medicine, show the positive impact summer programs can have on kids in every domain, and the effect is cumulative. It builds year over year and helps millions of kids catch up, keep up, and propel forward into the school year ahead.

Together, and with the guidance from this book and its authors, we can ensure summer is a transformative time for all children to explore new adventures and learn on their own terms, with libraries playing a critical role in their growth, safety, and well-being. What Brett and Liz have also achieved is to help showcase that summer is a springboard for year-round learning. This book is filled with activities first tried in their award-winning summer program, but then embraced year-round by the librarians in Chicago.

At the National Summer Learning Association (NSLA), we gave our Founder's Award to the Chicago Public Library (CPL) for the impactful partnership between CPL and the Museum of Science and Industry for the redesign of summer reading to summer learning and for their work to integrate STEM (science, technology, engineering, and mathematics) and literacy. This has sparked a national movement in libraries that we at NSLA are proud to support.

Pairing STEAM with Stories is the product of seven years of amazing work in Chicago. What Brett and Liz have done together is to combine the best of current science education principles with some of the finest books available for youth today into a model that works in many types of summer programs. When we pair books with science learning, we increase the access to both and make important connections that help reduce barriers and broaden learning.

When a strong partnership is formed for the right reasons, incredible outcomes can be realized. This has been true between these two organizations, and this volume represents the second book to spring from this work. But this book and its predecessor are representational of the real outcome of this partnership: hundreds of thousands of children's lives have been made better through fun and engaging science and literacy experiences across Chicago, and now they are being shared nationally. When you do this type of work you can watch youths *learn how to learn* while connecting what they already know to their new knowledge. We at NSLA look forward to sharing and promoting the valuable lessons and information in this book with our partner educators and allies nationwide. Together, we can ensure that all youths, regardless of background and zip code, can access, afford, and benefit from the supports they need to learn, grow, and thrive all year long. This is powerful learning, and it is through good partnerships, a shared vision, and collective will that we can harness summer to help all children grow and thrive.

I know you will enjoy these experiences and so will the youths and families you serve all year around. Thank you for your inspiring work.

AARON DWORKIN, CEO
National Summer Learning Association

ACKNOWLEDGMENTS

LIZ: This body of work would not be possible without the wonderful kids and families of Chicago who participate in the Summer Learning Challenge with us each year. I would like to thank the incredible group of people who comprise the Children's Services and Family Engagement team of Chicago Public Library. You have been my colleagues, my friends, and champions of this work—and me—from day one. You are the most amazing group of people, and I will always look at the time we worked together as the best time of my life. Here's to Caroline Broeren, Cristina Camargo, George Coleman, Jason Driver, Katie Eckert, Josh Farnum, Lori Frumkin, Alexa Hamilton, Liv Hanson, Shilo Jefferson, John Mangahas, Noemi Morales, Becca Ruidl, and Aldo Vasquez. Thanks to everyone at Chicago Public Library, including the CPL Board of Directors led by Linda Johnson Rice; Commissioner Andrea Telli; Mary Ellen Messner, Michelle Frisque, Craig Davis, Patrick Molloy, Scott Mitchell, Amaris Marshall, Andrew Medlar, Mark Andersen, and so many others who support this work; and to the absolutely best children's librarians there are: Children's Services Librarians and Associates of CPL. To Brian Bannon, who led CPL during the redesign of our program: your belief and encouragement will always be remembered. For my coauthor and friend, Brett Nicholas, who brings such joy to our partnership: your unending energy, support, and good humor are matched only by your professionalism, intellect, and friendship. The Museum of Science and Industry (MSI) Community Initiatives Team is a wonderful group of colleagues and co-conspirators, and we love working with you. We wouldn't be where we are today without the vision, commitment, and friendship of Bryan Wunar, who is foundational to every aspect of this effort. And I'd like to extend my gratitude to the MSI staff under David Mosena for their generosity and partnership to all of us at CPL. Steve Musgrave, illustrator and friend for so many years: I am humbled by your gifts to the library each year, in summer and year-round, and for your friendship. Gratitude to the Chicago Public Library Foundation staff and board, the best advocates for children in Chicago, who continue to support our work and who have been so kind to me in my career. Dr. Matthew Boulay, Aaron Dworkin, Laura Johnson, Maleka Lawrence, and everyone at the National Summer Learning Association: thank you for believing in the public library as a place of immense learning opportunities and for your work to drive equity, opportunity, and access for America's kids. Jamie Santoro, editor extraordinaire: without you believing in us, we wouldn't have this work; thank you for always being so gracious and supportive and for being my friend. To the members of the Association for Library Service to Children's Summer/Out-of-School-Time Learning Task

Force for going on this national adventure with me: thank you. Thanks also to Susan Benton, Jennifer Blenkle, and the staff of Urban Libraries Council for your vision and strong voice in supporting libraries as places of learning in summer. Gratitude for patient friends who have supported me and seen what I see for kids and learning, especially Fred Cribbett, Karen and Pat McAuliffe, Gerry Labedz, Amy Twito, and Cindy Wells. And, always, to my family, Steve, Maren, and Phoebe: you are everything.

BRETT: I would like to thank the entire Museum of Science and Industry community and their continuing commitment to the mission set forth by our founder, Julius Rosenwald: "To inspire the inventive genius in everyone." Those words continue to guide the work of my colleagues at MSI without whom this work wouldn't be possible. Thank you to the outstanding Community Initiatives Team of Angelina Mendoza, Gail Hutchison, Lorianne Willis, Rudy Albsmeyer, and Zändra Chisolm-El. It is an honor to work with people who are both incredibly talented educators and committed change makers dedicated to bringing science to life for youths in out-of-school settings. David Mosena, president and CEO of MSI, thank you for seeing the value and providing the resources to support informal science in nontraditional spaces like libraries and after-school organizations. To current and former leaders in the Education and Guest Services Division, thank you for providing support and a stable structure that has allowed this work to thrive and evolve. Andrea Ingram, Mary Krinock, and Rabiah Mayas, none of this work would have succeeded without your passion, vision, and advocacy. A special thank-you to my friend Julie Parente, whose simple idea of providing instructions for STEM activities to help families have fun learning during the summer blossomed into one of the most impactful programs the museum has for out-of-school-time audiences. Thanks for making sure we are keeping these activities accessible and fun by using your two wonderful kids as market research consultants and public relations models. To Bryan Wunar, your vision made the expansion of this program, and by extension this book, possible. Thank you for your mentorship and guidance. So many people have brainstormed, prototyped, and improved these activities over the years that it is impossible to thank everyone. It has truly been a collaborative effort. Keith Hand, Kylie Kosulic, Marvin McClure, Patrick McCarthy, Carla Thacker, and Ruth Goehmann: thank you for all of the great ideas and suggestions; you make prototyping my favorite part of this process. To the hardest working, most dedicated person I have ever had the pleasure of working with, Liz McChesney: thank you for being you! You have opened my eyes to the passion of librarians and the power of libraries as community anchors. Our conversations are always inspiring! My passion for science and reading started with my parents, and my younger siblings were my inspiration to become a teacher. Thanks for setting me up for success. And, of course, all my love to my brilliant and beautiful partner in life and all things, April Chancellor, and our wonderful son, Arthur. You mean the world to me.

INTRODUCTION
Are We Reaching Everyone?

In 2012, the Chicago Public Library Children's Services team debriefed from our summer reading program, paused, and asked ourselves this question: Are we reaching everyone? We had a robust summer reading program that ran like a well-oiled machine. Why tinker with it? Because the concept of inclusion is a North Star for librarians serving youth. As a career-long children's librarian and new director at one of the largest library systems in America, in my heart, I already knew the answer about reach. Then I was proved right: there was a large untapped population of kids who didn't choose or couldn't come to the library for summer reading. There were the obvious physical limits to our reach, though we helped shatter some of those barriers with the formation of a mobile STEAM (science, technology, engineering, the arts, and mathematics) and early literacy outreach team named the STEAM Team. But there were also kids who just didn't come to us in the public library. The Children's Services team and I found that some of these youths were kids who really like to draw or build or play sports, and some were kids who like science or coding, and a lot of the kids who weren't coming to the library were youths who didn't feel good about their reading ability or who did not particularly like to read. To them, summer reading was not an enticement to visit us or participate in our program. This new approach is a way to build equity in our communities and our library offerings. We increase participation in our summer program by engaging more kids in more neighborhoods and with new learning styles. The Summer Learning Challenge increases access to and participation in reading, STEAM learning, and family engagement across Chicago.

In Chicago, we set out to widen access to the types of library learning we offered, and we wanted to stop the summer slide. *Summer slide* is the name given to the gap in opportunity for youth. This gap is especially steep for those children who are living in poverty. Research collected from the National Summer Learning Association shows that children in poverty have less access to high-quality programs in the summertime. By missing opportunities to continue structured learning during the summer, children fall behind their more resourced peers. Armed with this knowledge, thinking about the kids we weren't serving through a reading-based program, and with a desire to deepen the impact the library makes on children, we set out to make a difference.

As in all libraries, learning of all sorts is happening in the Chicago Public Library (CPL): STEAM learning, art programs, music, citizen science, cooking—the list goes on and on. To laser focus ourselves, we set out to understand more about learning theories and to open our program to the strategic twenty-first-century skills that are essential for kids to succeed in a fast-changing world. The four Cs of twenty-first-century learning—creativity, communication, critical thinking, and collaboration—are critical for the ability to succeed in any setting. We also wanted to align our program to the priorities of the library's strategy. We tested and pushed ourselves, developed important partnerships that we have sustained through the years, and learned how to rigorously evaluate. What we found is that summer matters. It matters a lot for all youth, and it matters all year long.

The most elemental partnership we formed is with the Museum of Science and Industry (MSI). Since 1933 the museum has been working to help educate children and families in science and to help create the next generation of science learners. Many education programs for different audiences are offered by MSI, but they all strive to make science relevant and meaningful. For youths and educators in out-of-school-time settings, the museum creates programs that focus on building capacity in individuals and organizations and reducing barriers to participation and that result in positive STEAM experiences as a key indicator of success. We reached out to the educators at MSI to help us think about STEAM as a strategy, not a theme, and the science educators and administrators answered that call through deep and sustained partnership. MSI and CPL have a meaningful partnership based on our mutual goals to create lifelong learners and support Chicago's children. We have done this through annualized professional development, cocreation of curriculum, and grants we now apply for together, and at the heart of it all, this comes from MSI's incredible generosity to CPL. This partnership is so effective because of the alignment of vision between the institutions. Libraries and museums both have a reach and depth of learning that can help fight learning inequity. Both institutions believe this to be true, and both are able to act on that imperative. By harnessing the knowledge, reach, and intention of both institutions, we set out to broaden access and opportunity. And now, through years of data analysis by the University of Chicago–Chapin Hall Research Collaborative, we have discovered that we can not only help stop summer slide, but also help kids make academic gains when they participate.

We looked to STEAM to help build critical twenty-first-century learning into the summer program. All too often we find that technology unto itself is called STEAM learning. While access to these new and emerging tools is essential, we felt that we had to step back and also think about ways of thinking that scientists employ. This allows us to focus learning and resources appropriately in the library. Considering the scientific habits of mind allows us to think about the traits and characteristics we want to develop in the next generation of science learners. Thinking like a scientist is very similar to the sorts of critical thinking we hope to inspire in our library users. At its core, this approach starts with asking meaningful questions that are based on learners' interests and observations. Then the learners are encouraged and supported to conduct careful investigations that put the ownership of learning on the children. Finally, participants communicate what they have learned to others and become able to make claims based on the evidence of their observations. Science, like reading, is not a static enterprise. Our understanding develops as we learn more and apply what we know. The process of reflection is critical to closing the learning cycle and is effective when applied to learning programs in libraries. Having the curiosity to ask why, the confidence to investigate and communicate, sets up children for success in school, work, and, most important, life.

STEM is a critical lens through which we can view the twenty-first-century skills our kids need and deserve. We added the *A*, making it STEAM, to include creativity and artistic expression, which are so important to scientific endeavors. Pairing STEAM with children's books also allows us to deepen the connections and build more intersections for learning. So, in partnership with the MSI Community Initiatives Team, CPL decided to use those letters, *S-T-E-A-M*, in a broader and bigger sense to build those dispositions of sound scientific reasoning and critical thinking, creating engaged learners and people who value education and learning. Laying the groundwork for building children's curiosity, skepticism, openness to learning, ability to persist in the face of failure, and interest in connecting learning from one subject to another is a meaningful place to be for the twenty-first-century library. In fact, we see STEAM learning as offering a set of tools that allows our kids to gain important skills necessary to being engaged and empathetic citizens. It combines the best of social-emotional learning with all the same skills we hope to build in information literacy. It equips children for deeper engagement with the tools and types of experiences they are likely to encounter later in their education and in life. Scientific thinking allows children to ask questions and solve problems in a way that is meaningful in their lives. These skills were what we wanted to bring alive for Chicago's children.

Both CPL and MSI believe that learning takes places in multiple ways and that combining books and hands-on activities is one way to accelerate understanding. Pairing fiction and nonfiction writing with STEAM is an effective way to build connections and expand reach for our audiences. Story sharing is a great entry point for STEAM learning. Stories help kids build empathy for characters, which can motivate them to find solutions based on science and engineering. We find that adding informational texts and resources to deepen a child's understanding makes the learning that much more powerful. We can then use hands-on activities to explore related science or engineering concepts.

This book combines some of our tried-and-true, fun-and-joyous science recipes for twenty-first-century learning. This is certainly not a comprehensive list, but it includes topics clustered around concepts that we have explored in Chicago at the library, in the museum, and in conducting outreach. Although we created these for summer, we use them year-round and hope you will too. Each activity uses a book as the entry point. With some activities, we have made the connections between the story and the science for you, and at other times we leave it for you to create your own book–science link. We believe in diverse and beautiful books as a way for children to see themselves and learn about the world around them. We believe it is important to *read, discover,* and *create.* We see it as a matter of equity and inclusion to build these skills with all children from all parts of our city. And we believe in the right of all children to have fun while they learn—something that these projects are intended to promote. We hope you enjoy exploring STEAM in your library through book connections.

Helpful definitions for science vocabulary are included with each activity, but keep in mind that these definitions are only a starting point. As learners gain experience with the concepts, more nuanced definitions can be explored. Eight activities are noted as being appropriate for use with preschool-age children, meaning those who are four to five years old. You will want to allow more time and consider more assistance with the activities when adapting to this audience. We have also included a Program Planning Rubric at the end of this book to help you find connections between your favorite books and STEAM elements. Note that we have also included a place for you to consider how participants may reflect on their learning. This is active learning, and we hope you will go on this learning voyage with the kids you serve. As with sitting at the reference desk and facing questions from patrons, you may not know all the answers, but you do know how to find them. Put that practice to life when you do STEAM activities with your young patrons. After all, the more you learn, the more you can do!

Chapter 1

Float Your Boat

Along the River **by Vanina Starkoff**

| 30–45 minutes | Preschool Activity |

LEARNING OBJECTIVE: Participants will experiment with buoyancy and determine how boat design impacts the amount of weight a boat can hold.

> **buoyancy.** *Buoyancy describes how well something floats.*

Floating and sinking are great concepts to explore with children of preschool age and older. In this project, your library participants will build, test, and redesign an aluminum foil boat to find the design that can hold the most pennies.

MATERIALS YOU WILL NEED

- large plastic tub or sink half filled with water
- aluminum foil (restaurant-style precut sheets work well, if you are able to purchase them)
- rulers (if you are measuring aluminum foil)
- several hundred pennies

SCIENCE IN THE LIBRARY

Boats are able to float in water because of buoyancy. Buoyancy is the upward push of a liquid on an object. Boats float because the water is pushing up on the boat more than the boat is pushing down on the water. When more weights—in this case, pennies—are added to the boat, the boat pushes down on the water more than the water pushes up on the boat, which causes the boat to sink.

This is a great experiment to introduce the concept of density to children. Density is a combination of how much something weighs and how much space it takes up. Something that is heavy and small, like a baseball, is denser than something that is light and large, like an inflated balloon.

INSTRUCTIONS

1. If you are using aluminum foil from a roll, measure out a piece of foil that is as long as it is wide. (Each piece of aluminum foil should be the same size so each boat is built from the same amount of material.)
2. Decide what design the boat will be. Will it be shaped like a canoe or a ship or a barge or something else?
3. Fold and shape the boat into the desired design.
4. Place the boat in the water and start adding pennies one by one. Count the pennies as they are added.
5. Continue to add pennies until the boat sinks. How many were added? Can the boat be redesigned to hold even more pennies?

> ◗ **Pro Tip**
> Leave room in your program time for children to redesign their boats and to talk about iteration, or trying something a second time based on what they learned the first time. The amount of independent work by participants should vary based on their age. Younger children will need more help.

Chapter 2

Slime Time

Bounce by Doreen Cronin or
Bartholomew and the Oobleck by Dr. Seuss

60 minutes	Preschool Activity

LEARNING OBJECTIVE: Participants will experiment with polymers to change glue into slime.

> **molecules.** *Molecules are groups of atoms bonded together. Atoms are the tiny bits of matter from which everything is made. There are many, many different types of atoms and molecules.*
> **polymers.** *Polymers are molecules bonded together and repeated over and over to make long chains.*

Slime is perhaps one of the most fascinating substances known to us, and it is fun to incorporate into a library program. But did you know, you can also change the slime recipe just enough to make a bouncy ball? Your programs will be energized with this second fun experiment!

MATERIALS YOU WILL NEED (PER PARTICIPANT)

- school glue
- Borax laundry additive
- water
- measuring cups and spoons
- craft sticks
- disposable cups
- food coloring
- bowl
- wax paper

SCIENCE IN THE LIBRARY

Glue, like rubber, is made of polymers, which are long chains of molecules. Glue turns into slime when all the polymers get linked together. Link the polymers in glue together with Borax to make slime, and then change the recipe to make a bouncy ball.

At first, the polymers in glue just slide past each other, but adding Borax causes a chemical reaction. Borax links those polymers to each other and connects them in a big network; this is called cross-linking. Now the polymers can't slide around, and the mix solidifies into slime. More Borax means more cross-linking, which makes the slime firmer.

INSTRUCTIONS

1. Measure one-half tablespoon of Borax and put it in a cup or bowl.
2. Add two tablespoons of water and stir. Not all of the Borax will dissolve.
3. In another cup or bowl, measure two tablespoons of glue and add two tablespoons of water.
4. Add a few drops of food coloring and stir well.
5. Quickly pour the Borax mixture into the glue mixture and stir rapidly. If you have a helper, one person can stir the glue while the other pours in the Borax. The mix should instantly turn to slime.
6. If you would like, add some glitter or other small items to the slime. Finish mixing by hand.
7. Try experimenting with other ratios of Borax, glue, and water to make slime of different consistencies. A hard bouncy ball can be made by mixing glue and Borax without water.

> ### ▶ Pro Tips
> Collect small bottles with lids, or use zippered sandwich bags to send participants home with a sample of their slime. Have hand wipes available for easy cleanup. You will also want to place a tarp on the floor to save your library's carpeting or flooring.

Chapter 3

Flying Gyroscope

Abuela **by Arthor Dorros** or
My Granny Went to Market **by Stella Blackstone**

45–60 minutes

LEARNING OBJECTIVE: Participants will learn how weight and spin can make an object fly through the air in a stable manner.

> **rotational inertia.** *Inertia means something in motion tends to stay in motion until a force slows it down. Rotational inertia means something spinning tends to keep spinning until a force slows it down.*

This is a great outdoor program. Try these flying gyroscopes in an open space where people won't be hit if one doesn't move exactly where you intended. After reading one of these books, discuss how a grandma *or* simple plastic tube can fly so far. The answer? With science! Or, more specifically, with rotational inertia. Then build and test this deceptively simple-looking toy that flies a lot farther than expected. How far can each child throw it?

MATERIALS YOU WILL NEED (PER PARTICIPANT)

- one-liter plastic soda bottle
- tape
- pennies
- ruler
- scissors with a sharp point
- marker
- utility knife (optional)

SCIENCE IN THE LIBRARY

Two things help the flying gyroscope fly so well: its shape and the weight from the pennies. As the tube flies, there is very little air resistance caused by its shape because the air goes right through the middle. That reduced friction helps the tube maintain its forward speed. The weight from the pennies affects how it spins. The spinning weight located on the leading edge keeps the gyroscope from tumbling. Imagine throwing a Frisbee without spinning it. It would tumble and fall quickly to the ground. The spinning motion, or rotational inertia, stabilizes it and keeps it flying.

INSTRUCTIONS

1. Provide a one-liter bottle with straight (not curved) sides for each child.
2. Draw a straight line all the way around the bottle near the bottom. Be sure the line is on a part of the bottle that has straight vertical sides.
3. Have an adult poke a hole on the line with the sharp point of the scissors or a utility knife. Cut all the way around the bottle, discarding the bottom.
4. Measure three inches from the first cut and draw another line around the bottle.
5. Have an adult poke a hole on this line with the scissors or a utility knife. Cut all the way around the bottle, discarding the top. You should be left with the middle piece of the bottle that is now a cylinder with straight sides.
6. Tape four pennies on one end of the tube so they are equally spaced apart.
7. To fly the gyroscope, hold it like a football. Throw it penny-side forward and give it a spin, the same way a football is thrown. You can also throw it underhand: grab it by the nonweighted end, throw it penny-side first, and put a spin on it. It may take you a few tries to get the hang of it! Make sure the gyroscope spins as it flies; that's what will help it travel farther.

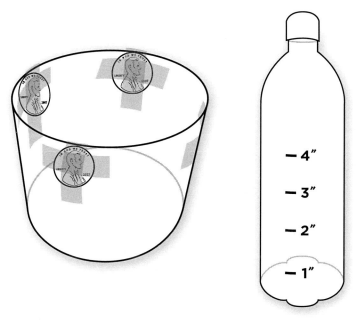

Chapter 4

See Cool Patterns with a Kaleidoscope

Yayoi Kusama: From Here to Infinity by Sarah Suzuki and
Kaleidoscope by Salina Yoon

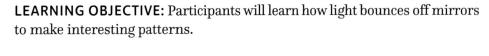

30 minutes

LEARNING OBJECTIVE: Participants will learn how light bounces off mirrors to make interesting patterns.

> **reflection.** Light bouncing off a surface is reflection. A mirror reflects light.

Chances are everyone here has looked in the mirror today, but have you ever thought about how your reflection appears? Reflections are visible when light bounces off a smooth, shiny surface and back into your eyes. But what happens when you look at the reflection of a mirror . . . in another mirror? Let's build a kaleidoscope to find out!

MATERIALS YOU WILL NEED

- cardboard pieces (either corrugated or thinner cardboard, but pliable enough to cut into a six-by-six-inch square)
- ruler
- tape
- paper (several sheets of copy paper for each participant)
- Mylar sheet (six-by-six inch square cut from an emergency blanket)
- scissors
- pencil
- glue
- markers of different colors

SCIENCE IN THE LIBRARY

Light bounces off all the objects in the world that you can see. Reflections happen when light bounces off a very smooth object, like a mirror. The smoother an object is, the clearer the reflection will be. Mylar sheets reflect better than aluminum foil, but mirrors reflect light even better.

INSTRUCTIONS

1. Cut a piece of cardboard into a six-by-six-inch square. Cut the Mylar into a six-by-six-inch square.
2. Determine which side of the Mylar is shinier, and glue the dull side to the cardboard. Try to have as few wrinkles as possible.
3. Cut the cardboard-Mylar into three rectangles that are each two inches by six inches.
4. Line up the cardboard pieces next to each other on a table so the long edges are touching and the Mylar sides are facing down. Space them so there is a small gap in between each rectangle. Tape the rectangles together along the long edges.
5. Flip the cardboard-Mylar over, so the shiny Mylar side is now facing up. Keep the middle rectangle flat, and fold the left and right rectangles up from the tape seams so they make a triangle. Tape those two sides together to hold that triangle shape.
6. Use markers to draw a design on a piece of white paper that is a little bigger than the open end of the cardboard triangle.
7. Cover one end of the kaleidoscope with the paper so the design faces inside and tape it in place. Look through the other end of the kaleidoscope. What patterns do you see?

> ⊙ **Pro Tips**
> Mylar sheets are sold at craft stores or sometimes in gift-wrapping sections of stores. Some stores sell plastic mirrors that can be cut or even precut rectangular glass mirrors. Using mirrors will produce an extremely clear, reflective surface for the kaleidoscope.

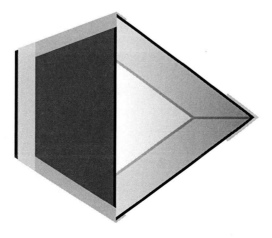

Chapter 5

Wacky Wobbler

***Mirette on the High Wire* by Emily Arnold McCully** or
***The Man Who Walked between the Towers* by Mordicai Gerstein**

30 minutes

LEARNING OBJECTIVE: Participants will learn about center of balance and then apply it to make a toy that can't be knocked over.

> **equilibrium.** *Equilibrium means things or forces are balanced on all sides.*
> **mass.** *Mass is how much stuff or matter something has.*

Balance is a fun concept for kids, and these two award-winning books help children think about the bravery required in high-wire walking. Put a rope on the floor to represent a high wire, and have kids pretend to walk across their own imaginary high wires, arms out, one foot in front of the other. Talk about balance and equilibrium and what it takes to maintain balance as you walk, even across the floor. Then, make a wobbler to explore concepts like mass and gravity.

MATERIALS YOU WILL NEED

- cup with rounded lid (like one from an iced coffee or other drink; one for each child)
- tape
- modeling clay (enough for each child to have about a one-inch ball)
- several heavy washers or nuts
- craft supplies, glue, and scissors (optional)

SCIENCE IN THE LIBRARY

Adding weight to the upside-down lid concentrates the mass in one spot, creating a low center of gravity. Gravity will pull the center of mass downward to the lowest possible point until the object is in equilibrium. Most of the wobbler's mass is in the washers, and the only way for it to be in equilibrium is when the wobbler is vertical. The rounded bottom allows for the unique wobble motion as the toy reaches equilibrium.

INSTRUCTIONS

1. Make sure the cup is empty and clean. Remove the rounded lid and use tape to cover the circular hole in the lid, being sure to cover the hole from both the inside and the outside of the lip.
2. Mold the clay into a ball about one-inch across, or a little smaller than a Ping-Pong ball. Place the ball of clay inside the lid, covering the hole that is taped shut. Place the weights directly into the center of the clay. Squish them down so they're secured tightly into the clay. If you're using multiple washers, tape them together first.
3. Keeping the lid upside down on a table, flip your cup over and carefully secure it into the lid. Don't compress the plastic lid—it needs to stay rounded and without any dents. Test it out! Gently push the wobbly cup to see if it stands back upright.
4. If you'd like, decorate your wobbler to make it into a silly creature, a pirate ship, or a monster to fit with other themes or books you may be using.

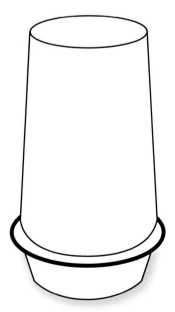

Chapter 6

Balance Bird

***Balancing Act* by Ellen Stoll Walsh** or
***So Light, So Heavy* by Susanne Strasser**

30 minutes

LEARNING OBJECTIVE: Participants will learn how to use center of gravity to make a toy bird that can balance on a fingertip.

> ***center of gravity.*** *The center of gravity is the point where all weight is evenly dispersed and all sides are balanced.*
> ***equilibrium.*** *Equilibrium means things or forces are balanced on all sides.*

Reading about balance is more fun when you also try it! These books about teeter-totters are a great entry to talking about how to balance an object. Birds move their wings to balance on the currents of air, so let's make a bird that helps us explore balance and equilibrium, or the state of opposing forces balancing each other out.

MATERIALS YOU WILL NEED

- cardstock
- balance bird template
- scissors
- straw
- pennies or washers for each participant
- tape
- crayons or markers

SCIENCE IN THE LIBRARY

For an object to balance, it needs to be supported directly underneath its center of gravity. The center of gravity is the point where all weight is evenly dispersed and all sides are balanced. Without the pennies, the bird can't be balanced on its beak because the center of gravity is near the middle of the bird. When the pennies are put on the wings, the center of gravity is now located at the tip of the beak and it can be balanced on a fingertip.

INSTRUCTIONS

1. Copy or trace the balance bird template onto a piece of cardstock. You can also use a file folder or cardboard from a cereal box. Just make sure the bird cutout doesn't have any folds or creases in it. Have children draw a design on or color the bird.
2. Try balancing the bird by putting the beak on your finger. Does it stay?
3. Fold the straw in half and tape it to the underside of the bird so the center of the straw is just behind the head and the bent sides extend under the wings.
4. Tape one penny near the tip of each wing on the underside of the bird. Try to put each penny the same distance from the edge on each side.
5. Flip the bird over. Place the tip of the bird's beak on your finger, and it should balance.

Chapter 7

Circle Spinners

***The Hula-Hoopin' Queen* by Thelma Lynne Godin** and
***Wiggle* by Doreen Cronin**

45 minutes

LEARNING OBJECTIVE: Participants will learn how adding weight to a top can make it spin for a long time.

> ***inertia.*** *Inertia means something in motion tends to stay in motion until a force slows it down.*

Fun to talk about and fun to do: follow the reading of these two books with some hula-hooping in your library! Then explore the science of spinning when you make a spinner kids can also use for a game and to experiment with balance and symmetry. See how mass can make this spinner keep going and going and going. Then check out the next activity to have even more spinning fun by making Toothpick Tops.

MATERIALS YOU WILL NEED

- cardboard from a cereal box (enough pieces so each participant can draw a six-inch circle)
- adhesive tape
- scissors
- pennies or washers for each child
- drawing compasses
- paper clips
- pencil

SCIENCE IN THE LIBRARY (FOR BOTH CIRCLE SPINNERS AND TOOTHPICK TOPS)

Newton's first law of motion states that an object in motion tends to stay in motion until friction or another force slows it down. This is inertia. This spinning toy demonstrates that concept with rotational motion. An important part of how an object spins is how much mass it has and how far that mass is from the center, or axis of rotation. Which spinning toy has most of its mass near the center? Which spins longer and is more stable?

INSTRUCTIONS

1. Cut the cereal box so you have a large flat piece of cardboard with no wrinkles.
2. Use a drawing compass to make a circle that is at least six inches in diameter. You could also trace around the base of a round container that's approximately six inches to make a circle.
3. Cut out the circle. Find the center of the circle by using a pencil to mark the point where two diameters (the longest lines that can be drawn across a circle) intersect.
4. Partially unfold a paper clip so that it's shaped like the number 4.
5. Poke the short arm of the paper clip through the center of the cardboard disc. This point is what your circle spins on. Tape the longer paper clip arm in place. If you'd like, decorate your cardboard disc.
6. Grab the paper clip loop on top of the disc and give it a spin! Tape four pennies to the edge of the disc so they are across from each other and the same distance from the center. Spin and observe what happens.

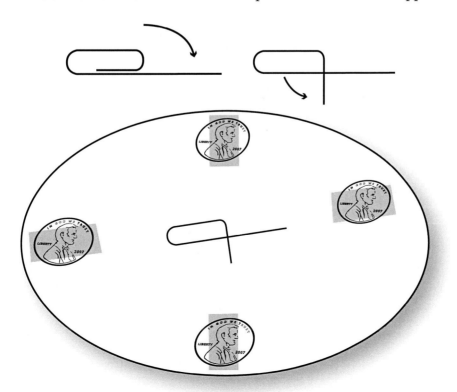

Chapter 8

Toothpick Tops

***The Hula-Hoopin' Queen* by Thelma Lynne Godin** and
***Wiggle* by Doreen Cronin**

30 Minutes

LEARNING OBJECTIVE: Build on what your program attendees learned during the Circle Spinners activity and discover what the best design is for a spinning toothpick top.

> ***inertia.*** *Inertia means something in motion tends to stay in motion until a force slows it down.*

Does it matter where the weight is distributed or how far off the ground it is? Experiment to make this top spin as long as you can.

MATERIALS YOU WILL NEED

- toothpicks (several for each participant)
- newspaper (a sheet or two for each participant)
- tape
- scissors

SCIENCE IN THE LIBRARY (FOR BOTH TOOTHPICK TOPS AND CIRCLE SPINNERS)

Newton's first law of motion states that an object in motion tends to stay in motion until friction or another force slows it down. This is inertia. This spinning toy demonstrates that concept with rotational motion. An important part of how an object spins is how much mass it has and how far that mass is from the center, or axis of rotation. Which spinning toy has most of its mass near the center? Which spins longer and is more stable?

INSTRUCTIONS

1. Cut long strips of paper that are one-half-inch wide.
2. Tape the strips together to make one strip that is at least three feet long.
3. Tape one end of your long paper strip close to one end of a toothpick, making sure the pointy tip is still exposed.
4. Wind the paper around the bottom of the toothpick, pulling the paper continuously to tighten it as you form a thick paper disc.
5. When you finish winding the last of the long paper strip, tape down the end.
6. Spin the paper-covered toothpick just like a top. How long does it spin? Try making a toothpick top with more or less paper and see how each change affects the way it spins.

Chapter 9

Straw Pipes

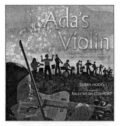

***Ada's Violin: The Story of the Recycled Orchestra of Paraguay*
by Susan Hood** or ***Zin! Zin! Zin! A Violin* by Lloyd Moss** or
***The Carnival of the Animals* by Jack Prelutsky**

60 minutes

LEARNING OBJECTIVE: Participants will learn how the length of a flute changes the note it makes.

> ***pitch.*** *Pitch is how low or high sounding a music note or other sound is.*
> ***vibration.*** *An object moving back and forth is vibrating. Even molecules in the air can vibrate!*

In *Ada's Violin*, Susan Hood gives us so many wonderful connections: make a collage based on the illustrations, create musical instruments using found objects, and explore sound! A great science connection to this is learning that sound always comes from a vibration. The speed of that vibration determines the pitch, or how high or low the sound is. Experiment with pitches by making different straw pipes. You can even play a song like Ada does. Pair this with *Zin! Zin! Zin! A Violin* to celebrate the beauty of the vibrations called music.

MATERIALS YOU WILL NEED

- thick straws
  (at least eight per participant)
- scissors
- tape
- ruler
- pen or marker

SCIENCE IN THE LIBRARY

As air is blown over the open end of the straw, it vibrates. The pitch is determined by the length of the tube, which acts as a resonating chamber. The longer the length, the lower the pitch or note. A long straw produces a low note, while a short straw produces a high note.

INSTRUCTIONS

1. Seal off one end of a straw by folding it over about one inch from the bottom and taping the end of the straw back onto itself. Tape the fold tightly so the fold stays in place. Check to see that the fold is airtight by blowing into the straw from the other end. Do this for three straws.
2. Cut the straws to different lengths.
3. Cut two pieces of straw that are one-inch long. These are the spacers.
4. Place a five-inch piece of tape on the table with the sticky side up. Lay down the straws on the tape in order from shortest to longest with a spacer straw in between each one. The tops of the straw pipes should extend a little above the tape line. Once all straws are in place, secure them with tape.
5. Place the straws so they are vertical and the open ends can rest on your bottom lip. Briskly blow over the open ends of each straw, experimenting with the angle to get the best sound.

As another activity, you can make a scale by cutting the straws to specific lengths. Fold and tape the ends of eight new straws. Measuring from the folds, cut the straws to the following lengths: 19.5 cm, 17 cm, 15.5 cm, 14.5 cm, 13 cm, 11.5 cm, 10 cm, and 9.5 cm. Number the straws from 1 to 8 with 1 being the longest straw and 8 being the shortest.

Try playing a song following the "notes" below. Or make up your own song!

Twinkle, Twinkle Little Star

11 55 66 5 44 33 22 155 44 33 2 55 44 33 211 55 66 5 44 33 22 1

> ⏵ **Pro Tips**
> Blow over the open ends of the straws the same way you would blow over a soda bottle. Straws with wider openings work better. If you use regular straws, it takes better aim to produce sound. Wider straws, often sold as smoothie or jumbo straws, can be found at superstores or purchased online.

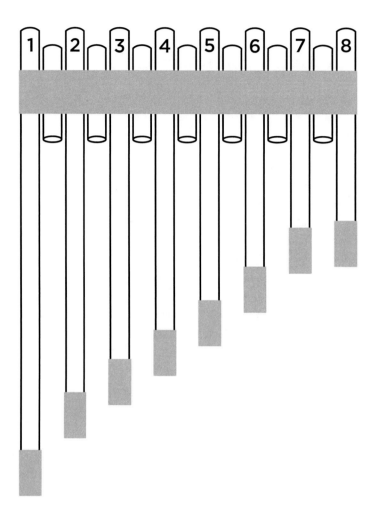

Chapter 10

Sound Sandwich

***Sounds All Around* by Wendy Pfeffer** or
***Trombone Shorty* by Troy Andrews**

| 30 minutes | Preschool Activity |

LEARNING OBJECTIVE: Participants will learn how sound comes from vibrations.

> ***vibration.*** *An object moving back and forth is vibrating. Even molecules in the air can vibrate!*

Use these beautiful books about music to learn about how sound is made. When you sing or hum, air passes over your vocal cords and makes them vibrate, or move back and forth really fast. There are lots of musical instruments that work this way, including this one, the Sound Sandwich.

MATERIALS YOU WILL NEED (PER PARTICIPANT)

- two wide rubber bands
- two jumbo craft sticks
- two smaller rubber bands
- scissors
- plastic straw

SCIENCE IN THE LIBRARY

When you blow through the sound sandwich, you can feel it vibrating against your lips. You just felt sound! Sound is produced when a vibration is transmitted through a solid, liquid, or gas. When you blow air through the space between the craft sticks, that air causes the rubber band to vibrate (move up and down quickly) between the two craft sticks. The vibration produces a sound.

Sound moves just like the rubber band, up and down in a wave. Sound waves can have different lengths, and different wavelengths result in different sounds. When the straws are placed closer together, the part of the rubber band that vibrates is shortened and moves more quickly, resulting in a higher-pitched sound.

INSTRUCTIONS

1. Place a wide rubber band lengthwise over one craft stick.
2. Cut two pieces of straw that measure about one inch each.
3. Tuck two straw pieces underneath the rubber band and slide each straw to opposite ends of the craft stick, about one inch from either end.
4. Place another craft stick on top of the straws, like the top piece of bread on a sandwich.
5. Wrap a smaller rubber band around both of the craft sticks on one end of the sandwich to hold it together. Use another rubber band to do the same on the other end. The rubber bands should pinch the two craft sticks together, and there should be a small space between the two craft sticks created by the two pieces of straw.
6. Hold the sound sandwich up to your mouth and blow through the space between the sticks.

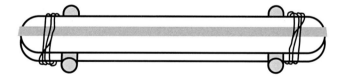

Chapter 11

Marker Tie-Dye

**Bloom: The Story of Fashion Designer Elsa Schiapparelli
by Kyo Maclear** or *Kente Colors* **by Debbi Chocolate**

30 minutes

LEARNING OBJECTIVE: Participants will make observations to determine what kinds of pigments are in different markers.

> **pattern.** *A pattern repeats in a predictable way or repeats over and over.*

Fabrics and designs are fascinating to kids! Take a patterned sheet or table-cloth for participants to sit on as they listen to these tales. Discuss patterns and go on a pattern scavenger hunt. Then, while learning about the science of color, make beautiful designs by separating the many pigments that are in permanent markers.

MATERIALS YOU WILL NEED

- white cotton fabric (pieces or whole shirts)
- permanent makers of different colors
- pipette or dropper
- rubbing alcohol
- rubber band
- cup
- hair dryer

SCIENCE IN THE LIBRARY

Permanent markers contain permanent ink, which does not wash away with water. However, the molecules of ink are soluble (capable of being dissolved) in rubbing alcohol. The rubbing alcohol carries the different colors of ink with it as it spreads in a circular pattern from the center of the fabric. Inks are usually mixtures of many different pigments, so you may see some colors separate out.

INSTRUCTIONS

1. Place a piece of cotton fabric over the opening of the cup.
2. Use a rubber band to secure the fabric in place, and pull the fabric tight.
3. Draw a design on the fabric with permanent markers. Round designs with open space work best.
4. With a pipette, place a few drops of rubbing alcohol in the center of your design. Watch as your design spreads!
5. Use a hair dryer to heat set your design and dry the rubbing alcohol.
6. Talk about what happened to the marker colors when the alcohol ran through them.

Chapter 12

Freaky Foam

***Yum! Yuck! A Foldout Book of People Sounds* by Linda Sue Park and Julia Durango**

| 30 minutes | Preschool Activity |

LEARNING OBJECTIVE: Participants will make this unusual substance so they can practice the science skills of observation and experimentation.

> ***non-Newtonian fluid.*** *Non-Newtonian fluids are liquids that don't act like water or regular liquids. They may flow differently or react to pressure differently.*

The universal expressions that we make are the fun foundation of this program. Kids can explore words from their own native languages and then link them to making this strange concoction that defies easy classification as a liquid or a solid but is very fun to play with and provides a great opportunity for scientific investigation.

MATERIALS YOU WILL NEED (FOR ONE BATCH TO BE SHARED PER PROGRAM)

- one and a half to two cups of cornstarch
- one cup of water
- one bowl
- spoons or craft sticks
- food coloring (optional)
- paper towels for cleanup

SCIENCE IN THE LIBRARY

Freaky foam is a suspension of cornstarch in water. It doesn't act like a normal liquid because it is a non-Newtonian fluid, which means that it changes how it moves when a force is applied to it. In other words, freaky foam acts like a solid when you punch it but like a liquid if you handle it gently. You can even jump on top of it if you create enough to fill a small kiddie pool.

INSTRUCTIONS

1. Pour the water into the bowl and gradually add the cornstarch while stirring. Be sure to scrape down the sides of the bowl to mix completely.
2. Start with one and a half cups cornstarch and add more as needed until the mixture becomes gooey.
3. Add food coloring if desired.
4. Play with the mixture.
5. Try to stir it slowly with your finger and then try to stir it fast. What happens?
6. Pick some up and squeeze it or shape it into a ball. Does it act like water or clay or something else?

> **◉ Pro Tips**
> This is an exceptionally messy project. These directions are written for a "batch" to be created as a demonstration with library staff leading. However, if you have the space and adult supervision, its always better for youth to have a direct hands-on learning experience.

Chapter 13

Rain Sticks

***Bringing the Rain to Kapiti Plain* by Verna Aardema** or
***Rain* by Manya Stojic**

60 minutes

LEARNING OBJECTIVE: Participants will learn how to make different sounds based on the materials used and how they are moved.

> ***vibration.*** *An object moving back and forth is vibrating. Even molecules in the air can vibrate!*

These two books elicit the sensation of rain on the parched earth. Rain and other weather events are experienced by everyone and every culture around the world. Telling stories of weather events is an important part of communicating observations of nature. Make a rain stick to tell your weather stories and do some weather reporting using sound and music. When we make these, we can explore the properties of sound. Does the rain sound soft or loud? Why?

MATERIALS YOU WILL NEED PER PARTICIPANT

- paper towel tube for each child
- 50–100 T-pins just a little shorter than the tube is wide
- two teaspoons of dried beans or seeds (lentils, bird seed, popcorn kernels)
- one-quarter cup uncooked rice
- duct tape or packing tape
- colored paper
- markers, ribbons, or crayons for decorating

> 🔒 **Safety Note**
> Rain sticks are meant for children three years and older because of sharp objects and swallowing hazards.

SCIENCE IN THE LIBRARY

As the beans and rice fall through the tube, they bump into the T-pins and make a sound. The sounds may be different depending on the number of T-pins used and the amount of rice and/or beans in the rain stick. Experiment with these variables to make different sounds. Traditional rain sticks are often made from natural materials like cactus, reeds, and bamboo. Some cultures use rain sticks in ceremonies and dances related to weather.

Sound is energy in the form of a vibration. Items such as seeds and rice when placed into tubes that are shaken create a sound that is like rain falling. A man named Jack Foley used items like rain sticks in his job at Universal Studios to simulate sounds (by using one object that sounds like another) in the movies. The people who do this for movie studios are now called Foley artists.

INSTRUCTIONS

1. Find the spiral seam that goes around the paper towel tube.
2. Push a T-pin through the seam about one-half inch from the end of the tube.
3. Continue pushing T-pins through the tube along the seam so they are no more than an inch apart from each other. (They can be closer.)
4. Once there are T-pins all along the length of the tube, tape one end shut so nothing can fall out.
5. Add a handful of beans and/or rice inside the tube and tape the other end shut.
6. Wrap the tube in colored paper and decorate it.
7. Tip the tube end over end and listen to the sounds. Can you make a sound similar to a gentle rain or a fierce storm?
8. Use the rain stick to tell each other stories about weather events you remember.

> ▶ **Pro Tip**
> Try using a wrapping paper tube or poster tube to make a longer rain stick. How does that change the sounds you can make?

Chapter 14

Far, Far Away

Magic School Bus Lost in the Solar System by Joanna Cole and Bruce Degen or **Super Cool Space Facts** by Dr. Bruce Betts

60 minutes

LEARNING OBJECTIVE: Participants will use scale to learn how far the planets are from each other.

> **scale:** *Making distances proportionally smaller.*

The distances between planets in our solar system are so great that they are hard to imagine. Help your kids understand the scope of this distance by building the solar system to scale using measurements and then having a race. Make this model to show the size of the solar system and how far all the planets are from each other.

MATERIALS YOU WILL NEED

- tape measure
- tape
- paper
- markers or crayons
- scissors
- craft sticks
- pictures of the planets/celestial bodies (optional)

SCIENCE IN THE LIBRARY

Our solar system includes the sun, eight planets, more than 140 moons, several dwarf planets like Pluto, asteroids, and comets. It takes about eight months for a spacecraft to reach Mars, which is 78 million kilometers (or 50 million miles) from Earth. Scientists believe the outer limit of the solar system is the

Oort Cloud, a spherical shell of icy objects. Planets nearby are much closer together, but once you pass Mars, everything is very far away.

INSTRUCTIONS

1. Make a marker for the sun, each of the planets, and Pluto. (Pluto may not be classified as a planet anymore, but it is part of our solar system.)
2. Write the name, and maybe add a picture, of each celestial body on a piece of paper.
3. Library grounds and rules permitting, you can do this as a race outside: tape a craft stick to each paper so you can stick it in the ground, and stabilize each sheet so that the paper stays upright.
4. Use the numbers in the following chart with any unit of measurement—steps, inches, feet, sidewalk squares, and so on. If your unit is a foot, measure one foot from the sun and place the marker for Mercury. For Venus, measure 1.8 feet (or 22 inches) from the sun or 0.8 feet (10 inches) from Mercury. Earth is 2.5 feet from the sun.
5. Once your solar system is set up, have a race. Who can get to Mars first? Who can race all the way to Pluto and back?

Planet/Celestial Body	Distance from the Sun	Distance to Next Planet/Celestial Body
Sun	–	1.0
Mercury	1.0	0.8
Venus	1.8	0.7
Earth	2.5	1.4
Mars	3.9	9.3
Jupiter	13.2	10.9
Saturn	24.1	24.4
Uranus	48.5	27.6
Neptune	76.1	23.9
Pluto	100.0	–

Chapter 15

Water Filter

***The Water Princess* by Susan Verde**

60 minutes

LEARNING OBJECTIVE: Participants will learn how water is cleaned by passing through different filters.

> ***filter.*** *To remove solid particles from a liquid.*

The water we drink comes from lakes, rivers, and underground aquifers but is filtered, cleaned, and treated before it gets to us. After reading *The Water Princess*, use an atlas or map to show where the water in your community originates. Where water comes from is important for children to know. Filtering water helps take impurities out of it and make it safe to drink.

In *The Water Princess*, Gie Gie must wait for her mother to boil water so it is safe to drink. Our water is purified too. But even when water looks clean, it is important for children to know it can still be dirty. The waste water we create is also filtered, cleaned, and treated before being returned to the environment. Make some dirty water and use different filtration techniques to see how clean looking it can get, and introduce the concept of water quality.

MATERIALS YOU WILL NEED

Note: You can use one bottle per child or just one bottle for a demonstration and group work project.

- plastic beverage bottle (a 1-liter or 20-ounce bottle is best)
- jar or vase that the plastic bottle fits into
- pitcher or another container
- scissors
- spoon
- measuring cup
- soil
- water

- items to use as a filter: gravel, sand, and cotton balls
- cooking oil
- cotton balls

SCIENCE IN THE LIBRARY

Water filters are used to remove impurities and solid particles from water to clean it. As the dirty water moves through the filter, each layer removes a different size or type of particle while letting the water molecules pass through. Once the water reaches the bottom, the filter has caught the debris and leaves clean, clear water. Each layer has a special job. The top gravel layer filters larger sediment and debris, like trash, rocks, and leaves. The sand layer filters fine impurities and organisms and can even help remove some bacteria and parasites. The cotton balls help remove any remaining contamination (like oil) that passed through the sand layer.

INSTRUCTIONS

1. Cut the bottom inch off the plastic beverage bottle and remove it. (Only an adult should do this.)
2. Turn the bottle upside down and place it in a jar or vase to hold it upright while you build the filter.
3. Make the bottom layer of your filter by adding cotton balls in the tapered end, packing them tightly in the bottom third of the bottle.
4. Add a little water to the cotton balls to help them stay packed and in place.
5. Next, add the sand to the filter, make the sand layer about three inches thick.
6. Finally, add a one-inch gravel layer, being sure to leave an inch of space above the gravel.
7. Pour one cup of clean water through the filter to wet the sand and cotton. Discard the water that comes out of the filter.
8. Make dirty water by filling a pitcher or container with about one liter of water. Add one cup of soil and stir thoroughly. Add a few drops of cooking oil and mix well. Now your water is ready to be filtered!
9. Slowly pour your dirty water in the filter one cup at a time. Wait until there is no standing water on top of the gravel before adding the next cup. Watch what happens as the water comes in contact with each layer of the filter. What do you notice? What does the water that drips out of the bottom of the filter look like? What do you think each layer is removing?

🔒 **Safety Note**
The water that comes out of your filter should be clearer and cleaner than it started, but it has not been treated for bacteria and is not safe to drink. Use this water for something like watering your plants.

Chapter 16

Weather Station— Anemometer

***The Weather Disaster* by Matthew McElligot** or
***I Face the Wind* by Vicki Cobb**

45 minutes

LEARNING OBJECTIVE: Participants will learn how to measure wind speed using an anemometer.

> ***anemometer.*** *An anemometer is a tool to measure how fast the wind is blowing.*

This is the first activity in a four-part series that you can run as a science club on weather or as four stand-alone programs. This activity can also be combined with the other three to make a weather station. Collect and compare data from your weather station to better understand the weather and make your own weather forecasts. An anemometer is an instrument that measures wind speed.

MATERIALS YOU WILL NEED (PER ANEMOMETER)

- string (approximately 12 inches long)
- Ping-Pong ball
- thermometer
- scissors
- tape
- protractor
- wind speed chart

SCIENCE IN THE LIBRARY

Weather describes the temperature, humidity, atmospheric pressure, wind, rainfall, and other meteorological characteristics of the atmosphere in a specific place at a specific moment in time. Different instruments help us measure all the different weather conditions. The anemometer measures wind speeds by moving a Ping-Pong ball on a string. When no wind is blowing the Ping-Pong ball should hang straight down, or vertically, but the faster the wind is blowing, the more the string will move away from that vertical position.

INSTRUCTIONS

1. Tape one end of a piece of string to a Ping-Pong ball and the other to the center of the straight edge of a protractor.
2. Hold the anemometer with the straight edge on top, parallel to the floor.
3. Note the angle of the string when the wind blows, and then use it to calculate the wind speed (see chart).

Angle	Wind Speed (km/hr)
90 °	0
95 °	9
100 °	13
105 °	16
110 °	19
115 °	21
120 °	24
125 °	26
130 °	29
135 °	31
140 °	34
145 °	37
150 °	41
155 °	46
160 °	52

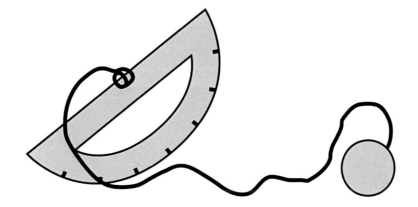

Chapter 17

Weather Station— Barometer

***Cloudy with a Chance of Meatballs* by Judi Barrett and Ronald Barrett**

45–60 minutes

LEARNING OBJECTIVE: Participants will learn how to measure atmospheric pressure using a barometer.

> ***atmospheric pressure.*** *Atmospheric pressure is a measurement of how hard the air above is pushing down on the Earth.*
> ***barometer.*** *A barometer is a tool to measure air pressure.*

This is the second activity in a four-part series that you can run as a science club on weather or as four stand-alone programs. This activity can also be combined with the other three to make a weather station. Collect and compare data from your weather station to better understand the weather and make your own weather forecasts. A barometer is an instrument that measures air pressure, which is the weight of the air molecules pressing down.

MATERIALS YOU WILL NEED (PER BAROMETER)

- small jar or cup (such as a yogurt cup or juice glass)
- balloon
- tape
- index card or piece of thick paper
- straw
- rubber band
- scissors

SCIENCE IN THE LIBRARY

Weather describes the temperature, humidity, atmospheric pressure, wind, rainfall, and other meteorological characteristics of the atmosphere in a specific place at a specific moment in time. Different instruments help us measure all the different weather conditions. The barometer measures air pressure. The straw pointing downward indicates low or falling pressure, which generally means a storm or rain is likely. The straw pointing upward indicates high or rising pressure, which generally means sunny weather.

INSTRUCTIONS

1. Cut the neck off a balloon.
2. Stretch the balloon over the top of a jar or small cup and secure it with a rubber band.
3. Cut a straw in half and trim at an angle to make a point.
4. Tape the straw to the balloon so the end is in the center and the pointed end extends over the edge of the jar. The tape should run along the full length of the part of the straw that's on the balloon, reaching to the edge of the jar.
5. Make a gauge by folding an index card in half so that it stands next to the straw. (The index card should be about twice as tall as the jar.)
6. Mark on the gauge the location where the straw points each day.

Chapter 18

Weather Station— Rain Gauge

Rain by Linda Ashman

30 minutes

LEARNING OBJECTIVE: Participants will learn how to measure rainfall using a rain gauge.

> **meteorology.** *Meteorology is the science of weather.*

This is the third activity in a four-part series that you can run as a science club on weather or as four stand-alone programs. This activity can also be combined with the other three to make a weather station. Collect and compare data from your weather station to better understand the weather and make your own weather forecasts. A rain gauge is an instrument used to measure rainfall.

MATERIALS YOU WILL NEED (PER RAIN GAUGE)

- plastic one- or two-liter bottle (with straight—not curved—sides)
- gravel (enough to fill the bottom of each bottle)
- ruler
- tape

SCIENCE IN THE LIBRARY

Weather describes the temperature, humidity, atmospheric pressure, wind, rainfall, and other meteorological characteristics of the atmosphere in a specific place at a specific moment in time. Instruments help measure the weather. A rain gauge measures how much rain falls at a time. The sides of the rain gauge need to be straight so each inch of measurement represents the same amount of water. The funnel helps keep other materials, like leaves, from getting in the rain gauge.

INSTRUCTIONS

1. Cut off the top fourth of a one- or two-liter bottle.
2. Add about two inches of gravel to the base of the bottle.
3. Tape a paper ruler on the outside of the bottle with the 0 mark at the top of the gravel.
4. Add water until it reaches the top of the gravel.
5. Make a funnel by inverting the top of the bottle that you cut off, placing it inside the base and covering the cut edges with tape.
6. After it rains, measure and record the rainfall amount on the ruler.

Chapter 19

Weather Station— Wind Vane

***Feel the Wind* by Arthur Dorros**

30 minutes

LEARNING OBJECTIVE: Participants will learn how to measure wind direction using a wind vane.

> **wind vane.** *A pointer that shows the direction of the wind.*

This is the fourth activity in a four-part series that you can run as a science club on weather or as four stand-alone programs. This activity can also be combined with the other three to make a weather station. Collect and compare data from your weather station to better understand the weather and make your own weather forecasts. Pair a fun story about a windy day with this wind vane activity that young children and school-age children alike will enjoy. A wind vane is an instrument that shows which way the wind is blowing.

MATERIALS YOU WILL NEED (PER WIND VANE)

- index card
- straw
- pushpin
- paper clip
- clay (enough to make a one-inch circle per wind vane)
- scissors

SCIENCE IN THE LIBRARY

Weather describes the temperature, humidity, atmospheric pressure, wind, rainfall, and other meteorological characteristics of the atmosphere in a specific place at a specific moment in time. Different instruments help us measure all the different weather conditions. The wind vane shows which direction the wind is blowing. Depending on where you live, the direction that the wind, and thus the weather, is coming from may help you predict how weather conditions will change.

INSTRUCTIONS

1. Cut an index card from corner to corner to make two triangles that are identical.
2. Cut the straw so it is the same length as the longest side of the index card triangles.
3. Use the pushpin to poke a hole in the straw at the midpoint.
4. Insert one end of a straightened paper clip into the hole and through the straw. The straw should spin freely on the paper clip.
4. Tape both triangles on opposite sides of the straw so the long sides of the triangles line up with the straw.
6. Tape the triangles together all along the meeting edge.
7. Poke a hole in the eraser on top of a pencil and insert the paper clip.
8. Use clay at the base of the pencil to hold the wind vane in place. The narrow tip should point in the direction the wind blows.

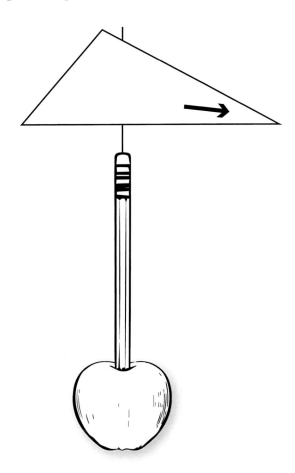

Chapter 20

Blown Over

The Wind Blew by Pat Hutchins or *Like a Windy Day* by Frank Asch

| 30 minutes | Preschool Activity |

LEARNING OBJECTIVE: Participants will learn how blasts of air can be controlled and aimed.

> *torus.* A torus is a shape like a donut or a tube with the ends connected to each other.

Create a balloon-powered cannon that blasts a stream of air powerful enough to knock down obstacles or create a gust of wind just like in these two picture books.

MATERIALS YOU WILL NEED (PER PARTICIPANT)

Note: An adult will need a utility knife and a dime to prepare the cups for the children's use.

- 16-ounce plastic cup
- large balloon (six inches in diameter or larger)
- marker
- scissors
- tape
- cotton balls

SCIENCE IN THE LIBRARY

When you snap the balloon, the air inside the cup is compressed and the only place for it to go is through the hole on the opposite end. As the air is forced through the hole, it makes a doughnut shape called a torus. This shape is created because the air leaves the hole at different speeds—the air at the center travels faster than the air at the outer edge, causing the outer edge of the moving air to roll backward on itself. According to Bernoulli's principle, the faster air moves, the lower its pressure.

The torus has higher pressure on the outside of the ring, which holds the shape together until it loses energy. If you fill the inside of the cup with fog from a fog machine, you can watch the torus travel across the room.

INSTRUCTIONS

Adult Preparation (per cup)

1. Place the cup upside down on your work surface and put the dime on the bottom of the cup in the middle.
2. Draw a circle around the dime.
3. Carefully cut the circle out using a utility knife.

Activity for Children

1. Fully inflate the balloon once or twice to stretch it out, but do not tie it off. This will make it easier to stretch later.
2. Use scissors to cut off the neck of the balloon.
3. Stretch the balloon over the top of the cup and tape it in place around the perimeter.
4. You should be able to pull the middle of the balloon back. When you let go of the balloon, a puff of air should shoot out the hole. This puff of air will travel straight for several feet.
5. Set up some lightweight targets, like cotton balls, and see if you can blow them away.
6. Make a pyramid with plastic cups or a tower of empty boxes. What's the heaviest thing you can knock over with the power of wind?
7. Place cups in a line. Can you aim the air cannon at one and knock it over without moving the others?

Chapter 21

Helping Hands

***Mousetronaut: Based on a (Partially) True Story* by Mark Kelly**

45–60 minutes

LEARNING OBJECTIVE: Participants will model a challenging situation to problem solve.

> ***astronaut.*** *A person trained to operate or work in a spacecraft.*

Think about Meteor the mousetronaut and how in space even a mouse needs a suit for protection from the cold, harsh environment. Astronauts making repairs to the International Space Station on space walks must wear gloves that protect them but allow their fingers to move easily. Have youths design their own space gloves and wear them as they try to use tools to complete various tasks.

The gloves that astronauts must wear while on a space walk are difficult to design. They need to be airtight for protection but also flexible so the astronauts can use their hands. Try having children wear some oversized gloves to do simple tasks so they see how difficult it can be to get the job done.

MATERIALS YOU WILL NEED (PER PARTICIPANT)

- tape
- rubber bands
- water
- large tub
- nuts
- bolts

- LEGO bricks
- pennies or other small weighted items
- tools: screwdrivers, pliers, or wrenches
- pairs of large plastic gloves (either dishwashing gloves or disposable medical gloves)
- aluminum foil
- plastic bags
- bubble wrap

SCIENCE IN THE LIBRARY

Astronaut gloves are even harder to maneuver than any gloves your participants could design. They're like inflated balloons, and the fingers resist bending. Astronauts must fight against that pressure just to use their hands, which can make them tired quickly and even cause injuries. Gloves are just one part of a space suit. Space suits provide astronauts with oxygen to breathe and water to drink while they're working in space.

INSTRUCTIONS

1. Put on an oversized pair of gloves and build a wall of LEGO bricks in 60 seconds.
2. Race against a friend to see who can build the tallest wall the fastest.
3. Make it more challenging by building a wall in just 30 seconds or using only the smallest LEGO bricks.
4. Fill a bin with cold water and put the tools, nuts, bolts, screws, and pennies inside.
5. Now make a pair of gloves that will keep your hands dry and warm while they're in the water using the tools. Be creative! Try layering different types of materials, or several different gloves.
6. Test your glove design by putting your hands in the water and using the tools. Thread a nut on a bolt, wind a screw with a screwdriver, and pick up pennies with pliers.
7. Try to complete all the tasks in the shortest amount of time. Make sure your hands remain underwater during the entire challenge!
8. When you're done, take off the gloves and see if your hands are dry and warm.

Chapter 22

On Your Mark, Get Set, Blow!

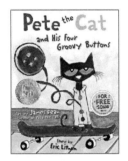

***Pete the Cat and His Four Groovy Buttons* by Eric Litwin**

| 45 minutes | Preschool Activity |

LEARNING OBJECTIVE: Explore the science of Newton's third law of motion.

> ***Newton's laws of motion.*** *Three scientific laws, written by Sir Isaac Newton, that describe how objects move.*

Pete the Cat loses his buttons when they burst from his shirt. Build balloon racers and explore the idea that for every action, there is an equal and opposite reaction, and use this to figure out why Pete's buttons fall off his shirt. Then, challenge someone to a race and experiment with different types of balloons.

MATERIALS YOU WILL NEED (PER PAIR OR TEAM OF AT LEAST 2)

- eight-inch-long piece of string for each team
- balloons (long skinny ones work best), one per team
- straws
- tape
- binder clips or clothespins

SCIENCE IN THE LIBRARY

As air rushes backward out of the balloon, it pushes the racer in the opposite direction with the same amount of force. This is Newton's third law of motion at work: for every action, there is an equal and opposite reaction.

INSTRUCTIONS

1. Team up into groups of at least two children who will together perform the following steps.
2. Take a piece of string, tape one end to a wall, and thread a straw on the string.
3. Blow up a balloon, close the end with a binder clip or clothespin, and tape it to the straw so that the neck of the balloon points in the opposite direction of the one the balloon will travel.
4. Hold the string so it's parallel to the floor, or even tape the other end to another wall.
5. Position the balloon racer at the end, remove the clip, and watch it go!

> ⊙ **Pro Tips**
> You can also race your balloons by setting up racetracks next to each other and challenging the teams to a race! Experiment with balloons of different sizes and shapes, or try making the racer go up a steep incline.

Chapter 23

Mind Reader Card Trick

***Mathemagic! Number Tricks* by Lynda Colgan**

60 minutes

LEARNING OBJECTIVE: Participants will see how algorithms can be used to create ordered patterns.

> **algorithm.** *An algorithm is a set of instructions used to reach a predictable result.*

Use this book as a place to jump into math learning in your programming. Kids can amaze their friends with their incredible mind-reading powers using this math-based predictive card trick.

MATERIALS YOU WILL NEED

- Decks of playing cards for every two children

SCIENCE IN THE LIBRARY

This trick uses an algorithm, or a specific set of steps that produces a predictable outcome. You deal out the cards in a way that organizes them and forces the selected card into a predictable position. When you repeat this pattern four times, the selected card always ends up in the exact middle of the deck. When the cards are dealt into columns, the card in the exact middle of the deck always ends up the fourth card down in the middle column.

INSTRUCTIONS

1. Pair up children into teams of two. One member of the team counts 21 cards from the deck and sets the rest aside before taking the following steps.
2. Ask your friend to pick a card from the deck of 21 cards and remember it but not tell you what it is.
3. Have your friend shuffle the deck of 21 cards and return it to you.
4. Deal the cards face up into three columns moving from left to right, with the cards overlapping. You should have seven cards in each column when you're done.
5. Ask your friend to point to the column the previously chosen card is in: left column, middle column, or right column.
6. Slide each column of cards together so they're in three stacks, keeping the cards in order as you slide them.
7. Make the three stacks into one deck again but in a specific order: make sure that the stack your friend pointed to is always collected second! This is very important to remember because it ensures that the column your friend pointed to is always placed in the middle of the deck.
8. Repeat the process: Deal the cards into three columns and ask your friend to point to the column with the previously chosen card. Make the columns into three stacks and pick up the stacks into one deck, making sure to pick up your friend's column second.
9. Repeat twice more, for a total of four times, leaving the cards in columns after the last time.
10. Reveal that your friend's card is the fourth card down in the middle column. It will be there every time!

Chapter 24

DIY Cloud

Little Cloud by Eric Carle

30 minutes

LEARNING OBJECTIVE: Participants will learn how temperature and pressure turn water vapor into clouds.

> ***air pressure.*** *Air pressure is a measure of how hard the air inside an object, like a balloon, is pushing outward.*

Clouds aren't always wanted, especially when they bring rain. But you can control the clouds yourself with this classic experiment.

🔒 **Safety Note**

Do this as a demonstration project because you will use a match. Make sure the matches remain in the hands of an adult and that they are not left where children can get them.

MATERIALS YOU WILL NEED

- one-liter plastic bottle with cap
- hot water
- measuring cup
- match

SCIENCE IN THE LIBRARY

This experiment creates a model of a cloud system in a bottle. How and when clouds form depends on a few factors, including temperature, air pressure, water vapor, and dust. The amount of water vapor that air can hold depends on temperature. In this experiment, you are changing the temperature inside the bottle with air pressure. Squeezing the bottle increases the air pressure and raises the temperature. Letting go makes the air pressure and temperature drop. With lower air pressure and temperature, water vapor comes together in tiny droplets and a cloud forms.

The smoke is added so there are tiny particles to give the water vapor a place to clump together. The fog you see is not from the smoke, but the smoke particles make the effect more dramatic.

INSTRUCTIONS

1. Make sure the plastic bottle is empty and clean.
2. Heat one cup of water so it is hot, but not boiling.
3. Hold the bottle upside down.
4. Carefully light a match and hold it under the opening of the bottle so the smoke rises into the bottle. Lift the match so it continues to burn while just inside the bottle. Blow out the match and capture the additional smoke in the bottle.
5. Turn the bottle and hold it slightly angled up so you can carefully pour the hot water into the bottle. Pour about half an inch of water in the bottom and tightly place the cap on the bottle.
6. Squeeze the bottle repeatedly. Does anything happen?
7. After several squeezes and releases, a cloud that looks like fog should form inside the bottle. When you squeeze the bottle, it should clear up and then become cloudy again when you release the pressure.

Chapter 25

Amped-Up Energy

Superhero ABC by Bob McLeod

30 minutes

LEARNING OBJECTIVE: Participants will use potential and kinetic energy to make a can appear to move by magic.

> **kinetic energy.** The energy an object has because of its motion.
> **potential energy.** The energy an object has because of its position.

After reading this book, introduce your superhero audience to their own superpowers: the ability to access science! Kids will astonish their friends by appearing to control objects with the power of their minds! Understand how potential and kinetic energy work to roll a can away from you and have it roll back to you in a predictable manner.

MATERIALS YOU WILL NEED (PER PARTICIPANT)

- round can with a lid, like an oatmeal canister
- twist tie
- hex nut, about one inch wide
- large rubber band
- two paper clips
- scissors
- nail
- paper, markers, and craft supplies

SCIENCE IN THE LIBRARY

To understand how the can works, you have to understand energy. Energy comes in many forms. One form of energy is motion, called kinetic energy. Another form is stored, or potential, energy. The can uses both forms. When you push the can, you give it kinetic energy and it moves away from you. The hex nut holds the middle of the rubber band still while the rolling can causes the ends to twist. The can rolls until the rubber band is completely twisted. This is when kinetic energy becomes potential energy—the can is not moving, but it has the ability to do so. Potential energy is stored in the twisted rubber band. As the rubber band unwinds, the potential energy again becomes kinetic energy and the can rolls back to you.

INSTRUCTIONS

1. Adult Preparation: Use a nail to make one hole in the center of the lid and one in the center of the bottom of the can.
2. Pinch the rubber band and fit a small loop of it through the hole in the bottom of the can.
3. Slip a paper clip through the loop so the rubber band will stay in place when pulled from the inside.
4. Pinch the other side of the rubber band and fit a small loop of it through the hole in the lid.
5. Secure it with a paper clip so the rubber band is stretched from lid to bottom inside the can.
6. Put the twist tie through the middle of the hex nut and twist it around the edge. You should have two "bunny ears" of equal length sticking up when you're done.
7. Ask a friend to hold the lid away from the can to stretch the rubber band.
8. Wrap each bunny ear around one side of the rubber band that runs through the inside of the can. The hex nut should hang from the middle of the two sides of the rubber band.
9. Put the lid back on. If the rubber band is loose, pull it through the hole and tie it to make it tighter.
10. Decorate the outside of the can creatively.
11. Place the can on the floor and gently roll it away from you. Watch what happens! Through trial and error, you can figure out the timing and predict when the can will start to roll back to you. Then trick your friends by saying, "Come back, can," and it will look like the can is doing what you tell it to do!

Chapter 26

Egg-stronaut

***After the Fall: How Humpty Dumpty Got Back Up Again* by Dan Santat**

60 minutes

LEARNING OBJECTIVE: Participants will learn to use engineering processes to design, build, test, and improve an egg lander.

> ***engineering.*** *Designing and building machines or structures to solve problems.*

Try to get Humpty to fall without cracking, or use this in a space-themed program to get your payload safely to the surface. NASA engineers use different strategies and materials to carefully land rovers and other equipment on planets they want to explore. Your challenge is to design and build a lander that protects a raw egg that's dropped from up high.

● Pro Tips for Planning
Although you can have kids work alone on this, it's fun to have them work in teams to design their lander together. You can even use ladders or balconies of various heights to drop your eggs. One library brought in a fire truck and had firefighters drop the eggs from the top of a fire ladder! This challenge gets everyone involved and having fun in the library, so if you can clear it ahead of time, try to do it in a public place.

MATERIALS YOU WILL NEED

- raw eggs, one per participant or team
- zip-seal bag
- disposable cups
- tape
- scissors

- various items to protect the egg: balloons, cotton balls, craft sticks, straws, rubber bands, clay, or anything else you may have
- paper
- pencil

SCIENCE IN THE LIBRARY

This is an engineering design challenge. There is a problem—how to drop an egg without breaking it—and a challenge—come up with a solution. An important aspect of engineering is to try multiple solutions for achieving success. Even if your egg survives the first drop, there are still improvements that can be made. If the capsule doesn't protect the egg, be sure to investigate what went wrong so that you can make a new and better capsule.

INSTRUCTIONS

1. Keep your egg-stronaut from breaking by designing and building a landing device. Use the engineering design cycle for this experiment: design your landing craft, test it to see if it works, change your design to make it better, and retest to get new results.
2. Collect your materials. You'll need an egg suit (zip-seal bag), landing capsule (disposable cup), some internal padding to protect the egg, and external protection to safely land your craft.
3. Design ideas on paper before starting to build. Get creative! The designs should have internal and external protections and maybe even a way to slow down the capsule as it falls.
4. Before building your capsule, enclose the egg in a zip-seal bag. That way, if anything goes wrong, the mess is contained.
5. Build your landing device and put your egg inside. Test out your device by dropping it from up high. If the egg doesn't crack, the design is a success! If the egg cracks, you should make changes to the design and retest it.

> ⏵ **More Pro Tips**
> You can give each team some play money (the same amount for each team) and then sell items such as balloons or masking tape or cotton balls. Some higher-level challenges: Can the kids make a successful design using few materials? Can the egg be dropped from an even higher distance?

☻ LIBRARIAN'S CORNER
Dropping Eggs and the Fun of Engineering in the Library

One of the most fun activities I've ever done with my library kids is the Egg Drop activity. There is just something so daring and thrilling about dropping things from heights, but add to it that it's a raw egg, and, well, WOW! Okay, I do put a tarp down and place the eggs in zip-closure bags to protect my library, but it's still electrifying for kids to get to do this in the library or right outside—whatever your case may be.

The Egg Drop activity can be used for a variety of ages, which is great too. I have done it as a family activity with parents helping to design a device to safely land their egg, and I often do it with kids anywhere from eight years old through high school. In fact, in summer it's fun to have teen volunteers facilitate this with school-age kids. With young kids, we may talk about a comparison of materials and what makes things drop; with school-age kids, we talk about gravity, force, and motion; and with everyone, we discuss materials, variables, and predictions and what those things mean. It's also easy to link books to this activity—everything from a certain nursery rhyme about an egg king to books about space travel.

I also really like how much science there is to this—that I can discuss and use books to help demonstrate these principles. I can talk a little about physics or materials science or even fluid dynamics. (I can talk about them when I have my library resources with me, that is!) We also talk about the design process with this activity: we plan, test, drop, and then tweak our designs based on observation. We do this with the full intention of the design process in front of us, to help kids learn about failure, persistence, and iteration. You can even provide a variety of materials along with play money and have kids buy the materials they want their group to use. This gives kids an even better chance of understanding real-life constraints.

The other thing I like about this program is that it is time flexible. If I have a class visiting for science fair projects, we do this activity and link it to experiments in books. We may do it as one big group with one egg, which takes about 20 minutes and is a great way to demonstrate science fair principles. In the summertime, we may do this as a hands-on group project (the best way to do it!), which can take up to 90 minutes.

No matter how you do this activity, you are bound to have squeals of delight and laughter from all the participants. It's fun and easy and a really awesome way to get those young hands and brains engaged.

LUCAS SIFUENTES
Chicago Public Library, Back of the Yards Branch

Chapter 27

Original Reaction

Science Fair Day by Lynn Plourde

30 Minutes

LEARNING OBJECTIVE: Discover the awesome power of oxygen with an oozing, foaming, and safe chemical reaction. Be prepared for a bit of a mess and lots of excitement!

> **catalase.** *A common enzyme in most living cells that converts hydrogen peroxide into water and oxygen.*
> **chemical reaction.** *When atoms or molecules are mixed, they change into different substances.*
> **chemistry.** *The science of atoms and molecules.*

Offering endless fun with this twist on a classic science fair project, Original Reaction can be an exciting demonstration or hands-on project, depending on the age and size of your program group. Link *Science Fair Day* to this project to bring the book to life and make Mrs. Shepherd proud.

MATERIALS YOU WILL NEED (PER EXPERIMENT)

- 3% hydrogen peroxide (household grade, the type used to clean minor cuts)
- plastic bottle with a narrow opening (like one for water or soda)
- liquid dish soap (about one tablespoon per bottle)
- dry yeast packets (one per bottle)
- measuring cups and spoons
- small cup
- plastic table covering and large aluminum foil pan
- water

SCIENCE IN THE LIBRARY

Hydrogen peroxide is a molecule that has two hydrogen atoms and two oxygen atoms (H_2O_2). That means it's like water (H_2O) but has extra oxygen. That extra oxygen atom is released when exposed to an enzyme called catalase that's found in most living organisms. When you pour hydrogen peroxide on a cut and it foams, all those little bubbles are oxygen being released by the catalase enzyme found in bacteria and on your own skin. The yeast in this experiment also has the catalase enzyme. The dish soap traps the oxygen bubbles and makes foam. The more oxygen that is released, the more foam that is made. Eventually the foam runs out of space and is forced to ooze out of the top of the bottle.

INSTRUCTIONS

1. Pour one cup of hydrogen peroxide into the bottle.
2. Add a good squirt (about one tablespoon) of dish soap and several drops of food coloring.
3. Gently mix these ingredients by swirling the bottle.
4. In a separate small cup, pour one pouch (about two teaspoons) of dry yeast and add two tablespoons of warm water. The temperature doesn't have to be exact, but the temperature you might use for a hot bath is good.
5. Mix these ingredients together with a spoon.
6. The next step will make a bit of a mess, so protect your surface by placing the bottle in a large aluminum foil pan and cover the table with a plastic table covering.
7. Pour all the yeast mixture into the bottle containing the hydrogen per-oxide solution. The peroxide should immediately create foam, filling the bottle and oozing out of the top.

Chapter 28

Up, Up, and Away

Hot Air: The (Mostly) True Story of the First Hot-Air Balloon Ride **by Marjorie Priceman**

45 minutes

LEARNING OBJECTIVE: Participants will work collaboratively to build a balloon that shows how density makes hot air rise.

> ***density.*** *The relationship of volume and mass for an object.*
> ***mass.*** *How much stuff or matter something has.*
> ***volume.*** *How much space something takes up.*

Pair this Caldecott Honor Book with an experiment to demonstrate exactly what happened on that first ride involving the sheep, the rooster, and the duck. Have the youths move some molecules as you explore thermal energy. Float to your destination as you build a tissue paper balloon and then use hot air to make it soar.

MATERIALS YOU WILL NEED

- six sheets of tissue paper (at least 18 inches wide and 24 inches long), per team
- glue stick
- scissors
- masking tape
- heat gun (a hair dryer will work, but not as well)

SCIENCE IN THE LIBRARY

You have probably heard that hot air rises, but why does that happen? Air takes up space, which you can see when a balloon is filled up with air. But air also has weight. Air is made up of molecules, and when you heat up those molecules, they move around faster and faster and fewer of them will fit in a space like your balloon. That means the air inside the balloon weighs less than the air around it (it has a lower density). Things with a lower density will float. When the air inside the balloon cools, the density of the air increases so the balloon comes back to the ground.

INSTRUCTIONS

1. Follow these instructions to make a box out of the six sheets of tissue paper.
2. Glue two sheets of tissue paper together on the long edge so they overlap by about half an inch. Be careful to not tear the tissue paper as you're gluing. (Your balloon can't have any holes in it for the experiment to work.)
3. Glue two more sheets along the long end of your first set so you have four tissue paper panels glued together, with each sheet overlapping the previous sheet by half an inch.
4. Cut the remaining two pieces of tissue paper into squares whose sides are equal to the short edge of a complete sheet of tissue paper.
5. Glue one edge of the square to the short, top edge of the first full-sized sheet, overlapping the paper by half an inch.
6. Now it gets a bit tricky because you need to give the balloon a three-dimensional shape out of the flat sheets of paper. Glue the remaining three edges of the square to the short edges of the remaining three full-size sheets, with the tissue paper overlapping by half an inch.
7. Glue the last two long edges together. The resulting shape should look like a rectangular box that's open on one end.
8. Take the second square and glue it along the remaining open edges, as you did on the top. When you are done, you should have a sealed, rectangular box with six sides. Check your seams to make sure they are sealed. (If you have any rips or holes, add a patch by cutting a small piece of scrap tissue paper and gluing it over the hole.)
9. Pick one corner of the box and cut a small hole that's big enough to fit the nozzle of the heat gun or hair dryer. Put masking tape around the edge of the hole to strengthen it.
10. To launch, gently flatten the balloon and fill it with hot air by putting the nozzle of the heat gun inside the hole. Have a team member help keep the balloon upright as it fills with air. Once it seems full, keep the hot air blowing for a bit longer to make sure it's thoroughly heated. Then turn off the heat gun and let go!

🔒 **Safety Note**
Be careful—the heat gun gets very hot and should only be operated by an adult!

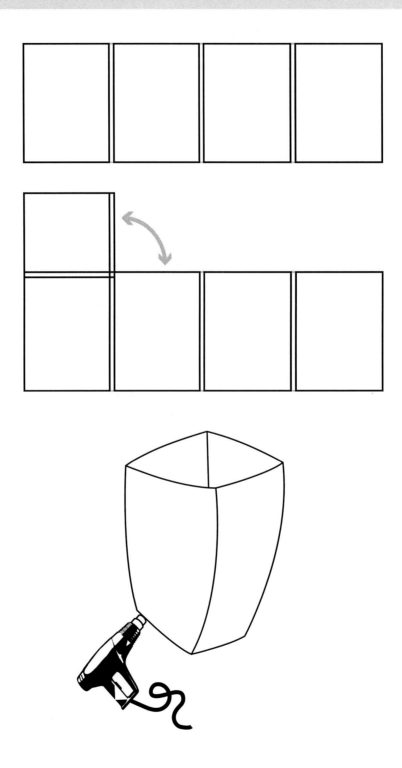

Chapter 29

Forget to Water Your Plants

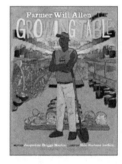

Farmer Will Allen and the Growing Table by Jacqueline Briggs Martin

45 minutes

LEARNING OBJECTIVE: Participants will see how plants can survive on just water and fresh air.

> **hydroponics.** _Growing plants in something other than soil._

Did you know that plants don't need soil to grow? Farmer Will Allen does! Share the success of this brilliant agriculturalist first in the book and then with this project. Build a simple hydroponic garden system in which water takes the place of soil and see if your plants grow faster and better. Try growing herbs or sprouting some beans for a yummy summer meal!

MATERIALS YOU WILL NEED (PER PARTICIPANT)

- yogurt cup
- small cup or can, slightly larger than the yogurt cup
- plant (e.g., ivy, pothos, herbs) or seeds
- cotton wick (can use a strip of T-shirt)
- perlite growing medium (available at garden stores)
- scissors
- tape
- water

SCIENCE IN THE LIBRARY

Plants don't need soil if there's a way for nutrients to go directly to the roots. In hydroponics, water takes the place of soil. Plants will often grow faster and better in hydroponic systems because the nutrients are delivered more efficiently. Hydroponics also eliminates soil pests and many diseases. In this system, water travels up the cotton wick to provide nutrients to the roots. NASA is experimenting with hydroponics to provide food on long-term space missions.

INSTRUCTIONS

1. Adult Preparation: Poke a small hole in the bottom of a yogurt cup with scissors.
2. Thoroughly wet a cotton wick in water and thread it through the hole, leaving several inches inside the cup.
3. Nestle the yogurt cup inside the larger cup or can and note how far down the yogurt cup reaches. If the yogurt cup touches the bottom, use tape to elevate it about an inch from the bottom.
4. Remove the yogurt cup and add water to your larger cup or can—keeping the water level below the bottom of the yogurt cup—and submerge the bottom of the wick.
5. Return the yogurt cup to inside the larger cup or can. Tape the yogurt cup in place if needed to keep it off the bottom.
6. Coil the wick throughout the growing medium as you add it to the yogurt cup so water will spread throughout.
7. If you're using a plant, gently clear the dirt from its roots before placing it in the yogurt cup, adjusting the growing medium to hold the plant upright. If you're using seeds, you can get them to sprout by burying them in the perlite.
8. If your cups are clear, cover the outside with paper; roots like to be in the dark.
9. Place your hydroponic garden in a sunny spot and add water to the larger cup when the level looks low.

> ◗ **Pro Tips**
> Some plants, like ivy, pothos, and spider plants, will grow in just water. Others, like lettuce and herbs, may wilt even though they're getting enough water from the wick. For a healthier plant, add nutrients to the water, like water-soluble plant food or nutrient solution made for hydroponic gardens.

Chapter 30

Two Scoops of Science

Ice Cream Summer by Peter Sís

45 minutes

LEARNING OBJECTIVE: Participants will learn about changing the properties of ice to make ice cream.

> ***freezing point.*** *The temperature at which a liquid turns into a solid.*

Pair this lovely read-aloud that shares the history of ice cream and how it is made with the actual food science behind ice cream. Food encompasses many different fields of science, from the botany of growing food to the chemistry of cooking to the biology of eating and digesting. Explore a little food chemistry by making your own ice cream.

MATERIALS YOU WILL NEED (PER PARTICIPANT)

- two to four cups of ice
- six tablespoons salt
- one tablespoon sugar
- one-quarter teaspoon vanilla
- one-quarter cup milk
- flavoring, like chocolate syrup or fruit juices (optional)
- zip-seal plastic bags in gallon and pint sizes
- measuring cups and spoons
- towel
- thermometer

SCIENCE IN THE LIBRARY

Water freezes and ice melts at a temperature of 32 degrees Fahrenheit (°F); this is called the freezing point. Salt can lower the freezing point of water to −22°F, meaning it needs to be colder than 32°F for water to freeze. That's why we put salt on icy sidewalks and roads in the winter; salt encourages the melting process. When you add salt to the bag of ice, it lowers the freezing point and the ice starts to melt as the temperature drops below 32°F. When you add the milk mixture bag to the bag of ice, heat leaves the milk bag and the temperature of the milk gets lower. Eventually the milk mixture freezes into ice cream!

INSTRUCTIONS

1. Fill a gallon-sized plastic bag halfway with ice, add six tablespoons of salt, and shake gently.
2. In a measuring cup, combine one-quarter cup milk, one tablespoon sugar, and one-quarter teaspoon vanilla and stir.
3. Add additional flavors using syrup, fruit juice, or candy, if you'd like.
4. Pour the milk mixture into a pint-sized zip-seal bag and seal it (getting as much air out as possible).
5. Put the milk mixture bag inside the big bag of ice and seal it.
6. Shake the bag for at least five minutes, wrapping it in a towel when it gets too cold, until it's frozen.

Chapter 31

Insulation Engineering Challenge

Ice Boy by David Ezra Stein

45 minutes

LEARNING OBJECTIVE: Participants will learn what kinds of insulation work well to keep an ice cube cold.

> **insulation.** *Insulation slows the transfer of heat energy so hot stays hot and cold stays cold.*

Insulation helps keep your house warm in the winter and cool in the summer, which reduces energy costs. Experiment with insulation to see how long your library kids can keep *Ice Boy* from melting.

MATERIALS YOU WILL NEED (PER PARTICIPANT)

- four small paper cups (three-ounce size)
- four clear plastic cups (16-ounce size)
- aluminum foil (enough so each participant can cover three cups)
- newspaper (enough so that every child can stuff a cup with a piece)
- felt, wool, or other fabric
- bubble wrap or other packaging materials (enough to wrap around the cups)
- one rubber band per child
- tape
- scissors
- four ice cubes that are the same size
- timer
- marker

SCIENCE IN THE LIBRARY

Insulators slow the transfer of energy from an object to its surroundings. They hold temperatures constant, keeping cold objects cold and warm objects warm. With good insulation, the speed at which an ice cube melts is slowed down. A good insulating material will not let heat energy from the outside reach the ice cube, so the ice cube stays cold. Insulation in your home works the same way. In the winter it keeps heat energy from leaving your home, and during the summer it keeps the outside heat energy from getting in.

INSTRUCTIONS

1. Cover the outside of one three-ounce paper cup with aluminum foil, trimming the foil to fit and taping it into place.
2. Cover another paper cup with newspaper in the same way.
3. Cover a third paper cup with a different material you would like to test.
4. Leave the fourth paper cup uncovered.
5. Place each paper cup into a 16-ounce plastic cup. If needed, add more insulation material to fill the gap between the cups.
6. Add an ice cube to each paper cup.
7. Cover the top of each plastic cup with plastic wrap, using a rubber band to hold the plastic wrap in place.
8. Put your cups in a warm place, like a sunny ledge, or place them in a shallow pan of warm water. This will help your experiment go faster.
9. Set a timer for five minutes.
10. Observe the cups and note how much water has melted.
11. Take the small cups out of the big cups and draw a line at the level of the melted water.
12. Place the small cups back into the larger cups, set the timer for another five minutes, and observe again. The insulator material that resulted in the least amount of melting worked the best. How long can you make an ice cube last?

Chapter 32

Newspaper Fortress

The Three Little Pigs and the Somewhat Bad Wolf by Mark Teague

45–60 minutes

LEARNING OBJECTIVE: Participants will learn how open-ended and collaborative design can be used to build a big structure.

> ***architect.*** *A person who designs buildings.*

Everyone needs a place they can call their own! Pair this classic story with some basic engineering skills to build a surprisingly strong fort out of seemingly flimsy materials like newspapers and masking tape. Can it keep out a somewhat bad wolf?

MATERIALS YOU WILL NEED

- newspaper, and a lot of it! (Aim for about two full Sunday editions per structure.)
- masking tape
- stapler and extra staples
- pencils
- sheets or plastic tablecloths (optional)
- pipe cleaners (optional)
- craft sticks (optional)

SCIENCE IN THE LIBRARY

Triangles are considered the strongest shape because they can handle heavy loads without collapsing. After you build your newspaper triangles, hold one and apply some force on the sides; the triangle should feel sturdy and hold its shape. If you put force on a square or rectangle, the shape can tilt or collapse. The triangle's strength is why architects often use it in structures. Bridges are made up of trusses, which are triangles that share sides and connections. Look for triangles the next time you see a bridge or a building being built. You will also find them in a geodesic dome, which is a spherical or partially spherical structure formed from triangles. You can find geodesic domes as part of climbing structures on playgrounds. Another example is the giant sphere at Epcot.

INSTRUCTIONS

1. Make newspaper rolls from two sheets of flat newspaper. Use open, two-page spreads, not single sheets. Roll them tightly—as tight as you can—from corner to corner; the tighter the roll, the stronger the support. Use a pencil to help start the roll, if needed. Place the pencil on the corner and roll the paper around it. Just be sure to take the pencil out once you get it started.
2. Secure the end with tape.
3. Use three newspaper rolls to make a triangle, attaching each corner with staples. Each triangle should be strong and not bent or folded. These triangles will be the basic units that you will use to construct your fortress.
4. Before building your fortress, decide what you want it to look like. It might help to sketch a design. How big will it be? Will you be able to go inside? Will the walls be covered? How many triangles will you need?
5. The newspaper triangles can be connected to each other in a lot of different ways using tape and staples. Try building flat walls or putting four triangles together to form a pyramid with triangle sides (a shape called a tetrahedron).
6. Once you get good at making triangles and tetrahedrons you can put them together in infinite ways to make whatever type of fortress you want!
7. Ask one or more people to help hold the pieces in place as you slowly construct your fortress. The structure will become sturdy and upright as you add layers and secure corners with tape, pipe cleaners, or even craft sticks.

> ### ⊙ Pro Tip
> This is an excellent small-group activity. Encourage kids to design and construct their fortress together, sharing ideas and working as a team to develop the sturdiest structure they can. It's a great way to encourage the twenty-first-century learning skills of communication, creativity, and collaboration.

Chapter 33

Seas the Day

Steamboat School by Deborah Hopkinson

45 minutes

LEARNING OBJECTIVE: Participants will use energy stored in a wound rubber band to power a boat.

> ***kinetic energy.*** *The energy an object has because of its motion.*
> ***potential energy.*** *The energy an object has because of its position.*

Put this powerful historical story into the context of what James's school looked like and felt like with this replica and learn about the science behind these boats. Steam-powered paddlewheel boats were common on American rivers in the 1800s, but now you're more likely to see smaller versions paddled by people. Both kinds work the same way, by pushing water with paddles mounted on wheels. Build your own boat that uses kinetic energy stored in rubber bands to move.

MATERIALS YOU WILL NEED (PER PARTICIPANT)

- cardboard, corrugated (enough to cut three pieces: one that is 5 inches by 10 inches, two that are 1.5 inches by 2.5 inches)
- rulers
- scissors
- duct tape
- rubber bands
- bin
- water

SCIENCE IN THE LIBRARY

When you wind up the paddle, the rubber band stores energy. This is potential energy, which occurs because the twisted rubber band is not in equilibrium—you have to hold it in place or it will unwind. When you let go of the paddle, the rubber bands unwind to rotate the paddle and push the boat forward. That unwinding is the conversion of potential energy to kinetic energy, which is the energy of motion. The rubber band moving the paddle, the paddle pushing on the water, and the boat moving forward are all examples of kinetic energy.

INSTRUCTIONS

1. Cut the cardboard into several pieces of these dimensions: one piece that is 5 inches by 10 inches and two pieces that are 1.5 inches by 2.5 inches each.
2. The large piece is the body of the boat. On one end of this piece, cut a rectangular window that measures three by four inches and is one inch from the edges. This is the back of the boat.
3. On the front of the boat, cut the corners on an angle so the front is pointed.
4. Cover the entire body of the boat with duct tape. This will help make it waterproof. The better you cover everything, especially the tricky inside corners, the longer your boat will last.
5. On each of the smaller cardboard pieces, in the center of the long edge, cut a slit that goes halfway through the piece.
6. Fit the two slits together in an X or plus sign shape. This is your paddle wheel.
7. Cover the X shape with duct tape.
8. To attach the paddle wheel to the boat body, stretch two rubber bands across the center of the boat's back window.
9. Place the paddle between the rubber bands, with one side of each rubber band placed on each of the four sides of the X.
10. Wind up the boat by turning the paddle backward.
11. Hold on to the paddle as you place the boat in water, and then let it go!

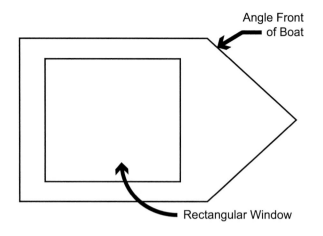

Angle Front of Boat

Rectangular Window

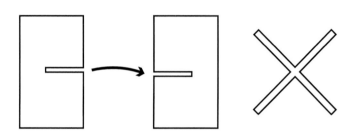

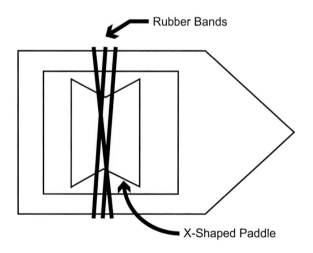

Rubber Bands

X-Shaped Paddle

Chapter 34

Look Out Below!

Parachute by Danny Parker and Matt Ottley

30 minutes

LEARNING OBJECTIVE: Participants will learn how to use air resistance to make a parachute land softly.

> *aerodynamics.* The study of how air moves and affects objects.
> *air resistance.* A type of friction from air pushing against an object.
> *payload.* The stuff that a flying vehicle carries, like cargo or passengers.

Build a parachute like the one Toby always wears in this story. Whether they are used for safety or sport, all parachutes work essentially the same way to help passengers land softly on the ground. Think like an engineer and design a parachute that lets you land your passenger safely on a target.

MATERIALS YOU WILL NEED

- string
- scissors
- tape
- binder clips
- pencil, markers, or crayons
- paper (one sheet per participant)
- pushpin (one per participant)
- toy figurine to be a passenger (one per participant)
- lightweight paper like tissue paper, napkins, or coffee filters

SCIENCE IN THE LIBRARY

Parachutes provide a lesson in air resistance. The broad surface area of the canopy catches the air and slows down the parachute. If you have ever flown a kite or tried to ride your bike into the wind, you know that air can push hard. Wind can push harder against something that has a broad, flat shape.

By experimenting with the weight, shape, and size of your parachute, you can change how fast and how much air is pushed out of the way. The study of how wind affects the speed of objects is called aerodynamics.

INSTRUCTIONS

1. Make a canopy by cutting a circle from a lightweight material (of the participant's choice).
2. Cut at least six pieces of string that are the same length.
3. Tape the string to the canopy at equal distances around the circle.
4. Tie the strings together at the other end.
5. Tie the binder clip to the bottom of the strings so a payload can be attached. Clip a toy figurine or other payload to the binder clip.
6. Draw a landing target on a piece of paper. Concentric circles in different colors work well.
7. Place the landing target on the ground and drop the parachute from a tall height. Did the parachute slow the fall of your passenger? Did the parachute go straight down?
8. Experiment to improve your parachute design. For the canopy, try different shapes, materials, and sizes. Some parachute canopies have small holes in them. Try more or fewer strings. What works best?
9. Try dropping the parachute from different heights and timing it as it falls to see which design is most effective.

> ⏵ **Pro Tip**
> There are many designs and shapes of parachutes, but all have a few common elements: a canopy that catches air, rope that hangs below, and a type of rigging to attach a payload or passenger. Use our suggestions to get started, and then experiment to figure out which parachute design works best.

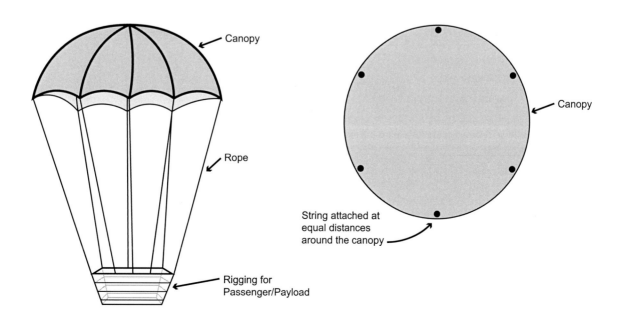

Canopy

Rope

Rigging for Passenger/Payload

Canopy

String attached at equal distances around the canopy

pH Rainbow

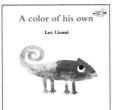

Planting a Rainbow **by Lois Ehlert or** ***A Color of His Own*** **by Leo Lionni**

60 minutes

LEARNING OBJECTIVE: Participants will learn to measure how acidic or basic different foods are.

> ***acid.*** *A type of chemical that can give a hydrogen ion.*
> ***base.*** *A type of chemical that can accept a hydrogen ion.*

We encounter acids and bases every day in the food we eat, like orange juice and milk, and in the household cleaners we use, such as bleach and vinegar. In chemistry, the pH scale tells you how acidic or basic a substance is. Make your own simple pH indicator and test the rainbow!

MATERIALS YOU WILL NEED

- red cabbage
- knife
- cutting board
- measuring cup
- measuring spoons
- boiling water
- two large bowls
- strainer
- several small cups
- sticky notes
- one-quarter cup of each substance to test (e.g., lemon juice, milk, club soda, vinegar, baking soda, soapy water)

SCIENCE IN THE LIBRARY

Scientists monitor the chemical and physical properties of natural water, like our rivers and lakes. Changes in pH levels and properties like acidity, temperature, density, and the concentration of different chemicals can have a profound impact on the health of the living organisms in the water. For example, organisms that use calcium carbonate to build shells—like oysters, clams, sea urchins, and corals—are especially sensitive to changes in pH levels. Conditions that are more acidic, or lower on the scale, make it harder for them to build shells.

> ◉ **Pro Tip for Planning**
> Gather old adult-size T-shirts or men's dress shirts or use smocks to cover kids' clothes before starting. The red cabbage stains, so you will also want to place a tarp on the floor in case of spills.

INSTRUCTIONS

1. Adult Preparation: Chop the cabbage into small pieces (about half an inch).
2. Place all the pieces in a large bowl.
3. Boil four cups of water.
4. Take the water off the heat and carefully pour the hot water over the cabbage.
5. Let the cabbage sit until it cools to room temperature.
6. Pour the mixture through a strainer and collect the liquid in a second container. This is your pH indicator. The color should be bright purple. Be careful, it can stain.
7. Prepare your substances for testing. Put about one-quarter cup of a substance into a small container and label it using a sticky note.
8. Repeat, placing substances in separate containers until you have all your samples ready. For powders like baking soda, mix one tablespoon into one-quarter cup of water.
9. Add a few tablespoons of the cabbage juice pH indicator to each small container and swirl.
10. Note the color of the cabbage juice, as this will change depending on how acidic or basic the substance is. A bright red or pink color means it is acidic. A purplish-blue color means it is neutral. A green or yellow color means it is basic. For exact color matches, find an online red cabbage indicator chart to use for comparison.

Chapter 36

Topsy-Turvy World

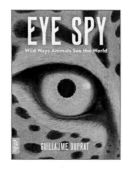

***Eye Spy: Wild Ways Animals See the World* by Guillaume Duprat**

60 Minutes

LEARNING OBJECTIVE: Participants will learn how light acts when it moves through a tiny hole.

> ***pinhole.*** *A tiny hole that lets light through.*

This book and experiment allow program participants to explore the properties of light and understand how the human eye works and then compare the human eye to the animal eyes in the Duprat book. Make a pinhole viewer to see the world in a new way—upside down!

MATERIALS YOU WILL NEED

- shoebox (one per participant)
- aluminum foil (enough to line the boxes)
- wax paper
- tape
- scissors
- pushpin

SCIENCE IN THE LIBRARY

The pinhole in the viewer acts like a camera lens, forcing light through to create an image on the opposite side. Light travels only in straight lines. When forced through a pinhole, only light from the top of the object you're seeing reaches the bottom of the paper in the viewer and only light from the bottom of the object reaches the top of the paper. The result is an inverted picture of what you're seeing. Your eye works like this too. Light travels through the lens and is reflected on the retina, the back of the inside of your eye. The image on the retina is also upside down; your brain just flips it right side up so you can tell what you're seeing.

INSTRUCTIONS

1. Cut two square holes on opposite ends of a square or rectangular box.
2. Cover one hole with aluminum foil and the other with wax paper, taping down the edges.
3. Make sure light doesn't get inside the box by taping off any gaps or edges.
4. Poke a small hole in the aluminum foil square with a pin.
5. Head outside or look out the window on a sunny day. Hold the viewer with the wax paper side facing you and look around. You'll see images reflected on the wax paper, but they're upside down!

> ● **Pro Tip**
> If your box is an extra-long shoebox, attach the wax paper inside in the middle of the box by taping a wax paper flap on either side. Get the wax paper as flat as possible. Hold the open side against your eye and block the sunlight with your hands as you look inside.

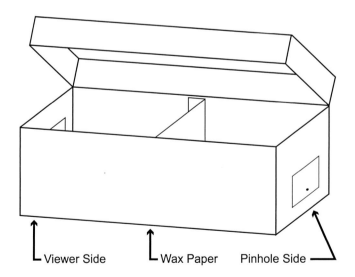

Viewer Side   Wax Paper   Pinhole Side

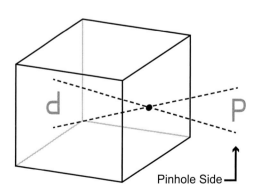

Pinhole Side

Chapter 37

Recycled Seed Paper

Seed! Seeds! Seeds! by Nancy Elizabeth Wallace

60 minutes

LEARNING OBJECTIVE: Participants will learn how to turn used paper into new paper. Participants will learn how seeds sprout.

> **cellulose.** *A polymer found in plant cells that is very tough.*

Paper is made from tree fiber or recycled from previously used paper. Go green and recycle used paper by making paper that will sprout into flowers when planted in the garden. Think about the seeds in this lovely book and consider other ways youths can learn from seeds.

MATERIALS YOU WILL NEED

- used paper (copy paper or lined paper works, about two sheets per child)
- two cups of water per sheet of paper
- blender
- measuring cup
- tablespoon
- pitcher
- spatula
- colander
- rolling pin
- cooling rack
- cheesecloth
- two towels
- food coloring
- small seeds (like wildflower or herb seeds)

SCIENCE IN THE LIBRARY

Fiber is a key part of making paper. Plant material contains the fiber cellulose, which is like the stringy bits of celery. Copy paper and other types of paper that are thin and perfectly smooth are made of small but strong fibers that interlock and stay together. When you blend paper with water and make pulp, all the fibers get broken up. When you pour the pulp onto cheesecloth and squeeze out all the extra water, the fibers interlock again and hold the paper together. Those fibers are also good at holding water. So, when you plant your seed paper and water it, the fibers hold the water so the seeds can sprout. The paper will naturally break down in the soil as your seeds grow into plants.

INSTRUCTIONS

1. Rip a sheet of paper into two-inch pieces.
2. Place the paper pieces in a blender and add two cups of water.
3. Blend the mixture until smooth. It should be very soupy.
4. Add a few drops of food coloring.
5. Pour the mixture into a pitcher and add a tablespoon of seeds.
6. Mix with a spatula.
7. Make a double layer of cheesecloth and place it in a colander.
8. Place the colander in a sink or large tub and pour the paper mixture through the cheesecloth-lined colander. The paper pulp should remain behind in the cheesecloth and the excess water should run through.
9. Gently press more water from the pulp using the spatula.
10. Lift out the cheesecloth and lay it flat on a towel.
11. Use a spatula to shape the paper pulp into a square or rectangle, if desired.
12. Place another double layer of cheesecloth on top of the paper pulp and another towel on top of that.
13. Press down on the top towel with a rolling pin to get out as much water as possible.
14. Remove the towels, take the paper out, and gently peel off the cheesecloth from both sides of the paper.
15. Place the paper on a cooling rack to let it dry overnight. You can try using a hair dryer on a low setting to speed up the drying process, but too much heat will damage the seeds.
16. Once the paper is completely dry, you can write, draw, and even paint on your paper. Create a postcard or a thank-you note.
17. You can even plant the paper in soil, keep it moist, and watch for the seeds to germinate and herbs or flowers to grow!

Chapter 38

Summer Slopes

***Teach Your Giraffe to Ski* by Viviane Elbee**

45 minutes

LEARNING OBJECTIVE: Participants will manipulate variables to control the motion of a marble.

> ***kinetic energy.*** *The energy an object has because of its motion.*
> ***potential energy.*** *The energy an object has because of its position.*

Try this twist on the giraffe who wants to ski down the biggest hill—also a variation of a classic arcade game. Experiment with variables of speed and height as you launch a marble down a ski jump to land in a target. Then build your math skills as you tally up your points!

MATERIALS YOU WILL NEED PER RAMP

- pool noodles
- two six-inch pieces of stiff wire or metal hanger
- duct tape
- marbles
- three empty cans
- chair

SCIENCE IN THE LIBRARY

Several types of energy are at work in the ski jump Skee-Ball. The marble has potential energy when it's sitting on the track, before it starts to roll downhill. As it rolls, the potential energy transforms to kinetic energy, or the energy of motion. Where the marble lands depends on two variables: how fast it is going when it leaves the ski jump and the angle at which it leaves. By changing these variables, you can aim for different cups. Find the optimal release point and launch angle for the marble by experimenting and making observations.

INSTRUCTIONS

1. To make the ski jump, cut the pool noodles in half lengthwise, so you have two pieces of track with a curved chute down the middle. (Only an adult should do this.)
2. Tape the tracks together to make one really long track. Be sure to put the tape on the outside of the pool noodle; if you put tape on the inside, it will cause friction and slow down the marble.
3. Carefully insert the wires into one end of the ski jump. (An adult should help with this.) The wires should be embedded in the foam material and parallel to the curved chute. These wires will allow you to bend the end of the jump to adjust it.
4. Get ready to play! Tape the top of the ski jump track high up on a wall, and prop up the curved end of the ski jump on a chair.
5. Set up the empty cans as targets.
6. To launch, place a marble at the top of the ski jump track and let it go. See if you can land a marble in one of the cups without bouncing it on the floor. How can you make the marble travel for a farther or shorter distance and land in a consistent spot?

> **◉ Pro Tip**
> This is a great project for youths to work on together in teams. Have the teams compete against each other on distance and speed.

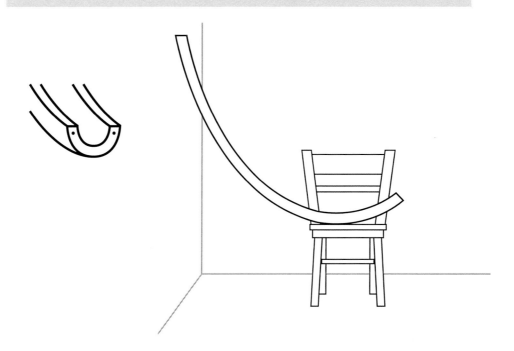

Chapter 39

Reach for the Skyscrapers

Iggy Peck, Architect by Andrea Beaty

60 minutes

LEARNING OBJECTIVE: Participants will build a structure though a process of open-ended design and continuous improvement in order to learn about dynamic loads.

> **architect.** *A person who designs buildings.*

Build your own skyscraper, fort, or personal book nook. Some planning, experimentation, and learning from mistakes will get you on your way to constructing buildings that can withstand all sorts of hazardous conditions—buildings that would make Iggy Peck proud!

MATERIALS YOU WILL NEED

- paper
- pencils, markers, or crayons
- newspaper
- tape
- disposable cups
- craft sticks
- straws
- glue
- card stock
- other building materials (blocks, toothpicks, fabric, etc.)

SCIENCE IN THE LIBRARY

When designing a building, engineers must consider the effect of forces that can change quickly; these are called *dynamic loads*. Earthquakes and wind are two examples of dynamic loads. Buildings must be flexible enough to absorb the force of wind but not so flexible that they sway from pressure on the top floors. Earthquakes create a sudden, severe change in force, so buildings must be constructed soundly to avoid collapsing.

INSTRUCTIONS

1. Draw the basic design of your favorite skyscraper. Consider the shapes that will help make your building strong.
2. Use a variety of materials to build a model of your design that is at least two feet tall and able to withstand winds and earthquakes.
3. When you're done, run a few tests:
    a. Aim a hair dryer or fan at the building as a wind test.
    b. Gently shake the table to simulate an earthquake.
    c. See how much weight your skyscraper can hold by stacking some small objects on top, like metal washers or wooden blocks, to see what it can withstand.
4. Consider how you may need to revise your design to make your skyscraper sturdier. Rebuild as needed and test again!

Chapter 40

Solar Snacks

Sun!: One in a Billion (Our Planet Series) by Stacy McAnulty

60 minutes

LEARNING OBJECTIVE: Participants will learn how light from the sun provides enough heat energy to cook food, specifically s'mores.

> **energy.** *The ability to do work like move an object or heat a substance.*

Almost all the energy on Earth comes from the sun, as the sun tells you himself in McAnulty's engaging biography. Solar energy is absorbed by the land, water, and atmosphere and is converted into heat that creates winds and currents in our atmosphere and oceans. Heat, or thermal energy, can be focused to create a solar oven that can cook food, a method you will try through this fun project.

MATERIALS YOU WILL NEED

- pizza box (one for a group or one each for participants)
- aluminum foil (enough to wrap the inside of the pizza box or boxes)
- plastic wrap
- tape
- scissors
- ruler
- paper plate
- s'mores ingredients: graham crackers, plain chocolate bars, large marshmallows
- hand wipes or paper towels for cleanup (after enjoying a snack!)

SCIENCE IN THE LIBRARY

The sun's light rays are collected by the foil flap and concentrated inside the box. The rays are transformed into thermal energy that slowly raises the temperature inside the box, causing the food to cook.

INSTRUCTIONS

1. About two inches from the edge of the pizza box lid, cut out three sides of a square.
2. Fold back the fourth side (the one you didn't cut) to create a flap.
3. Cover the inside of the flap with foil, shiny side out, taping it in place.
4. Open the box and cover the bottom and sides with foil. Cover the hole in the box lid that the flap made with plastic wrap, taping it in place.
5. Assemble a s'more:
    a. Start with half a graham cracker as the base.
    b. Add a square of chocolate and a large marshmallow.
    c. Finish with the other half of the graham cracker.
6. Put the s'more on a paper plate and place it inside the box on the foil bottom.
7. Close the lid, fold back the flap and prop it open with a ruler.
8. Put the box outside, with the flap facing the sun. Try to angle the box and the lid so as much light as possible is focused on the food.
9. The length of time it takes for your food to heat up depends on how much solar energy it is getting, so be patient! (The marshmallow might not brown, but the chocolate should melt a bit.)

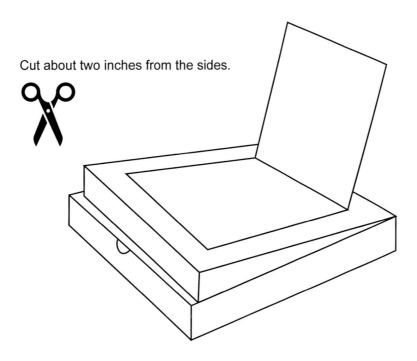

Cut about two inches from the sides.

Chapter 41

Stomp Rockets

Astro Girl by Ken Wilson-Max

30 minutes, but allow more time for participants to continue to launch	Preschool Activity

LEARNING OBJECTIVE: Participants will manipulate air pressure to launch a rocket.

> **compress.** *To squish down and make smaller.*

In *Astro Girl*, Astrid wants to be an astronaut more than anything else. Turn your library patrons into rocket scientists themselves as they launch rockets with these fun and easy stomp rockets.

MATERIALS YOU WILL NEED

Launcher
- Pool noodle (at least 1 per 5 participants)
- three pieces of PVC tube, one inch in diameter and six inches long
- two-liter bottle (1 per pool noodle)
- duct tape

Rockets
- clear tape
- 1 PVC tube per 5 participants to roll paper around
- paper (one sheet per participant)
- Ping-pong ball (one per participant)
- Markers or other decorating supplies to share

MARKERS OR OTHER DECORATING TO SHARESCIENCE IN THE LIBRARY

When you stomp on the bottle, you compress, or squish, the air inside. This compressed air must go somewhere, so it escapes through the easiest way out—the other end of the launcher. When you place the rocket over the other opening, this escaping air pushes it out of the way! The harder you stomp on the bottle, the quicker the air escapes and the faster the rocket is forced off the tube.

INSTRUCTIONS

1. Roll a piece of paper around the PVC tube to make a paper tube. Make sure the paper tube is loose enough to slide on and off the PVC easily.
2. Tape the paper to itself with clear tape so it holds its shape.
3. Take the paper off the PVC and attach the Ping-Pong ball to one end using clear tape. Wrap tape around the area where the tube and ball connect so no air can escape. This will be the rocket.
4. Decorate it to look like a rocket, a daredevil, a superhero, or anything else that flies!
5. Build the launcher by inserting the mouth of the two-liter bottle into one end of the pool noodle and securing it thoroughly with duct tape; make it as airtight as possible.
6. Insert the PVC tube into the other end, leaving half of the tube sticking out of the pool noodle.
7. Load the rocket onto the PVC tube.
8. Place the two-liter bottle on the ground and aim the launcher. It may be easier to ask a partner to hold the launcher for you.
9. Stomp on the bottle to watch the rocket fly!
10. To launch again, just blow forcefully into the tube to reinflate the bottle.

> ▶ **Pro Tip**
> This is so much fun that you will want to allow extra time in your program for attendees to try this again and again. Make sure you have a big room or go outdoors to launch stomp rockets. Be sure to keep kids out of the path of flying rockets. Be sure to have an adult aim the launcher to help keep lights and other objects inside the library safe.

☺ LIBRARIAN'S CORNER
Rocketing into Learning

Summer learning is all about capturing and channeling the powerful imaginations of our learners and using that mighty force to propel them into a summer of exploration, inquiry, and creation. In that sense, it is very much like rocketry, a topic that has proven itself to be the perfect opener for our Summer Learning Challenge.

Channeling the energy of children at play is as much a physical exercise as a mental one, and you'll always get your best results when you can find a way to combine the two. At Chicago Public Library, we use a stomp rocket activity as a low-resource, visually evocative, and fun way to engage learners and get them ready for summer learning. You can use this activity to teach your learners about important science concepts like force, propulsion, and kinetic energy. On a more abstract level, you can use stomp rockets to explain how repetition and observation are central to the scientific method. The greatest takeaway from this project, however, is that science is physical, tangible, and relatable—not just something that can be understood, but something your own body can create!

Stomp rockets are created from simple materials—leftover soda bottles, a length of PVC pipe and a pool noodle, and of course the rocket itself—just some nicely decorated paper and tape to seal it tight. Individually, these materials don't seem to have much significance, and that mundanity is central to why we perform this experiment. Getting our learners to activate their imagination and see the potential in everyday objects is a key goal of our programming. Once a child looks at a soda bottle and sees *energy* or *propulsion*, you've transformed imagination into invention.

The magic (really, the science) happens when you blend physical engagement with that inventive mind-set. When a rocket soars across your learning space powered by the mighty stomp of an energetic eight-year-old, you aren't simply teaching students about the transfer of energy or the movement of gasses. You are showing your learners how their bodies and minds can work together to change the world. That spark will send any kid rocketing into summer learning!

GREG DIAZ
Chicago Public Library, South Chicago Branch

Chapter 42

Bridging the Gap

Secret Engineer: How Emily Roebling Built the Brooklyn Bridge
by Rachel Dougherty

45 minutes

LEARNING OBJECTIVE: Participants will learn how triangles can be used to make strong structures, like bridges.

> ***load.*** *The weight or force pushing down on a structure.*

Emily Roebling helped her husband build the famous Brooklyn Bridge. Travel is always easier when you have a bridge to help you get across a rushing river or huge gorge that's in your path. There are many different bridge designs, but they all have the same function: to provide passage over an obstacle.

MATERIALS YOU WILL NEED (PER PARTICIPANT)

- nonbendy straws
- clear tape
- scissors
- ruler
- small cup
- two chairs or tables
- 200 pennies or metal washers to use as weights

SCIENCE IN THE LIBRARY

Look at a steel or wooden bridge and often you will see triangle shapes making up most of the bridge's support structure. These are called truss bridges. Triangles are structurally the strongest shape because they allow weight to be spread evenly throughout a structure, allowing it to support heavy loads. Truss patterns are used in other structures as well, such as roofs, radio towers, crane arms, and more. Engineers must consider loads, or the weights and forces that a structure must withstand. The dead load of a structure is the weight of the structure itself. The dead load of a bridge includes beams, cables, and the deck. The live load of a structure is the weight that is added to the structure, including people, cars, and wind.

INSTRUCTIONS

1. Before you build, come up with an idea of how you will design a bridge that is at least one foot long. Draw sketches if it helps you think through your ideas.
2. Build your bridge using only straws and clear tape.
3. When you are satisfied with your bridge, place it between two tables or chairs that are one foot apart.
4. Place the cup in the middle and add a few pennies at a time.
5. Count the pennies as you add them, and keep adding pennies until the bridge collapses. How many pennies did it hold? How did the bridge break? Can you change your design to make it stronger?

> **◉ Pro Tip**
> For an additional program element, turn this into a challenge by limiting the amount of straws or having the bridge span a distance longer than one foot. Have youth work in teams to practice collaborative problem solving.

Chapter 43

Bubble Blowout

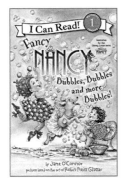

Fancy Nancy: Bubbles, Bubbles and More Bubbles! by Jane O'Connor

45 minutes	Preschool Activity

LEARNING OBJECTIVE: Participants will learn about the chemistry and shape of bubbles.

> **molecules.** *Molecules are groups of atoms bonded together. Atoms are the tiny bits of matter from which everything is made. There are many, many different types of atoms and molecules.*

This bubble solution lets you make huge bubbles that like to linger and are worthy of Fancy Nancy! Experiment with the shape and size of bubbles as you design your own wands, make a colorful bubble snake, and try to make giant bubbles—three projects in one!

MATERIALS YOU WILL NEED (PER PARTICIPANT)

- one cup warm water
- two tablespoons dish soap (original blue Dawn works best)
- one tablespoon glycerin
- one teaspoon sugar
- food coloring
- container with lid
- measuring spoons and cups
- scissors
- pipe cleaners
- straws

- tape
- cotton string
- one skein of cotton yarn
- two dowel rods or sticks
- beads (optional)

SCIENCE IN THE LIBRARY

A bubble is a thin film of soapy water filled with air. The soapy film is made up of three layers: one layer of water molecules sandwiched between two layers of soap molecules. Billions of these molecules will stick together to form the spherical shape of a bubble. No matter what your wand looks like, a bubble will always take on the shape of a sphere. The sphere shape minimizes the surface area of the bubble, which makes it the easiest shape to form using the least amount of energy. Adding glycerin and sugar to the bubble solution helps the bubbles last longer. The water in bubbles evaporates quickly, which makes the bubbles pop. Adding glycerin and sugar slows evaporation, which makes bubbles last longer.

INSTRUCTIONS

Bubble Solution

1. Mix together one cup warm water, two tablespoons dish soap, one tablespoon glycerin, and one teaspoon sugar.
2. Stir thoroughly and store for at least an hour in a covered container. When you're ready to try your bubble solution, gently swirl the mix in the container in case ingredients have separated.

Basic Wand

1. Design your own bubble wand using pipe cleaners. Be creative!
2. Bend the loop into different shapes.
3. If you'd like, decorate the handle with beads.
4. Let the wand absorb the bubble solution for a few seconds, and then blow your bubbles!

Bubble Window

1. Thread a piece of string through two straws and tie the ends together.
2. Position the straws so they are opposite each other, forming a square.
3. Hold the straws together and dip the "window" into the bubble solution.
4. Lift it out with the straws still touching and then re-form the square, this time with a bubble inside!

5. Blow gently or move your arms to make a huge bubble.
6. Experiment with different lengths of string to see how big of a bubble you can make.

Giant Bubble Wand

1. Use yarn to make two braids, one that's 18 inches long and another that's 36 inches.
2. Tape one end of the long braid to the end of one dowel, and tape the other end to the other dowel.
3. Tape the shorter braid in the same way on the same end of the dowel. Both braids should form a loop with the shorter braid at the top and the longer braid at the bottom.
4. Dip the wand into the bubble solution and let the yarn soak up plenty of solution.
5. Lift out the wand and slowly move it around to create huge bubbles!

Chapter 44

Signal the Superhero

***Lucía the Luchadora* by Cynthia Leonor Garza**

30 minutes

LEARNING OBJECTIVE: Participants will learn how shadows change based on how far away the light is from the wall.

> ***reflect.*** *When light bounces off a mirror or bright surface instead of being absorbed.*

As Lucía knows, every superhero needs to be easily recognized. Things like masks, costumes, and symbols help people in distress know who is there to save them. Create your own personal signal and let it shine high in the sky!

MATERIALS YOU WILL NEED (PER PARTICIPANT)

- paper towel tube
- packing tape
- paper
- pen or pencil
- rubber band
- scissors
- flashlight with a single LED (phone flashlights work well)

SCIENCE IN THE LIBRARY

As the light passes through the design, a shadow will be cast on the opposite wall. Using a flashlight with a single LED means all the light is coming from one source, so the light is concentrated and the edges of the shadows are crisp. A traditional flashlight with a reflective back will make the edges fuzzy, and that effect is intensified the farther away the light is from the wall.

INSTRUCTIONS

1. First, design a symbol that represents your superhero. Your symbol should be simple, easily recognizable, and representative of your super-hero identity.
2. Cut a square piece of paper that is bigger than the open end of the paper towel tube.
3. Draw your design in the center of that paper so that it's smaller than the diameter of the tube.
4. Cut out your design.
5. Keep your design from ripping by placing clear packing tape on both sides.
6. Place the design over the end of the paper towel tube with the design centered.
7. Hold it in place with a rubber band.
8. Turn off the lights and shine a flashlight through the other end to see the projection of your superhero signal on the wall.
9. Try moving closer to or farther away from the wall. What happens to the size of the signal on the wall? How far can you cast the signal and still have it be clear?

> **▶ Pro Tip**
> You can also do a reverse image of your signal by placing packing tape on the paper that surrounded the design you cut out, so that the center shape is empty and the light shines through.

Chapter 45

Cool under Pressure

Fire Boat: The Heroic Adventure of the John J. Harvey
by Maira Kalman

30 minutes

LEARNING OBJECTIVE: Participants will learn about the force of water, called water pressure.

> **pressure.** *A force applied over an area.*

Witness the never-ending struggle as air and water battle it out to equalize the pressure in an enclosed container as you make your own water blaster similar to the heroic hoses of the fire boats.

MATERIALS YOU WILL NEED (PER PARTICIPANT)

- two feet of one-inch PVC pipe
- PVC pipe end cap
- three feet of one-inch dowel rod
- expanding glue (like Gorilla Glue)
- metal washer (smaller than one inch)
- wood screw
- screwdriver
- handheld drill and one-quarter-inch drill bit (for adult use only)
- small piece of pool noodle
- bucket of water to load the blaster

SCIENCE IN THE LIBRARY

The blaster works by using pressure. When you put the blaster in the water and pull back, the pressure on the water outside the PVC pipe pushes the water into the empty pipe. This happens because you are increasing the volume, or space, inside the blaster and stretching out the air trapped inside. Think of the trapped air as a spring: when you stretch out the air, it is going to try to return to its original size. The only way it can do that is by drawing up water inside the blaster.

INSTRUCTIONS

The blaster has two parts: the housing (PVC pipe and cap) and the plunger (a pool noodle plug attached to a dowel rod).

1. Make the housing by gluing the PVC pipe to the cap with an expanding glue and following the directions to let it dry.
2. Once the housing is dry, have an adult drill a hole in the middle of the PVC end cap; this is your blast nozzle. (A small hole will shoot water farther while a large one will drench someone quickly! A one-quarter-inch drill bit produces a good middle ground.)
3. Make the plunger plug by having an adult cut a two-inch piece of pool noodle so that it lies flat.
4. Firmly press the open end of the PVC pipe onto the pool noodle until you see an impression of the pipe.
5. Cut around the impression so that your piece is slightly bigger than the inside of the PVC pipe.
6. Test to see if it fits firmly in the end of the PVC, and don't be shy about making new ones.
7. Place the pool noodle plug on one end of the dowel.
8. Put a washer on top of the plug, and then screw the washer and plug to the end of the dowel.
9. To use, put the plunger into the housing and push it almost all the way to the end.
10. Put the capped end of the PVC pipe into a pail of water and pull back on the plunger. If you have a good seal with the pool noodle plug, the water should not drip out of the nozzle.
11. Aim the blaster, push the plunger, and soak the world!

> ● **Pro Tip**
> The pool noodle plug in the piston blaster will eventually get worn out. When that happens, remove the old one and attach a new one.

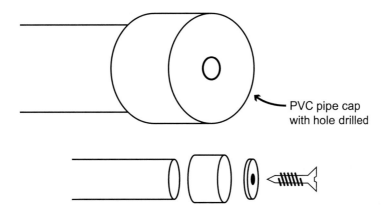

PVC pipe cap
with hole drilled

Chapter 46

Outta This World

Leave Me Alone! by Vera Brosgol

30 minutes

LEARNING OBJECTIVE: Participants will learn that pressurized air can push water fast enough to launch a rocket.

> **Newton's laws of motion.** *Three scientific laws, written by Sir Isaac Newton, that describe how objects move.*
> **pressure.** *A force applied over an area.*

In this funny book, Grandmother is on a quest to finish her knitting. Can you help her? Your mission is to help her get to space with a rocket launch. Pump air through a water-filled bottle rocket to create enough pressure to push the rocket skyward. Stand back so you don't get soaked on liftoff!

MATERIALS YOU WILL NEED (PER PARTICIPANT OR TEAM)

- two-liter bottle
- natural bottle cork
- 18-ounce plastic cup
- tape
- water
- scissors

- materials to decorate your rocket (paper, markers, ribbon)
- bike pump with needle adaptor (only one to be reused for each team)

SCIENCE IN THE LIBRARY

The water rocket demonstrates two basic science concepts: air pressure and Newton's third law of motion. By forcing air into a confined space, you are increasing the air pressure inside the bottle. This happens all the time—when you open a bottle of soda, the *pffft* you hear is pressurized air escaping. When you force air into the bottle, the pressure builds until something must give. In this case, the cork shoots out of the bottom of the bottle and the pressurized air forces the water out. This causes the bottle rocket to lift off per Newton's third law of motion, which says that for every action there is an equal and opposite reaction. The water shooting out of the bottom is the action, and the bottle flying up is the opposite reaction.

INSTRUCTIONS

1. Make sure the cork fits snugly in the bottle opening.
2. Cut the cork in half horizontally—most corks are longer than the bike pump needle, and the needle needs to reach all the way through the cork.
3. Force the needle through the cork and make sure air can pass through; you may need to pick some cork bits out of the needle.
4. Attach the needle to the bike pump nozzle.
5. Prepare your rocket by turning the bottle upside down and removing the label.
6. The bottle opening will be the base of the rocket, so add a paper nose cone to the bottom of the bottle (which will point up) and tape paper fins to the sides.
7. Turn the plastic cup into a launch pad by cutting a hole about two inches by one inch on one side of the cup near the bottom. The hole should be big enough for the cork and bike pump nozzle to fit through.
8. If the edges of the hole are sharp, cover them with tape.
9. Slide the bike pump nozzle with the cork on it through the hole.
10. Fill the rocket one-third to one-half full with water (this is a variable you can change later to see how it affects your rocket).
11. Fit the cork very snugly into the bottle opening. Turn the bottle upside down—it shouldn't leak—and place it onto the cup, with the bike pump tube extending through the hole in the side of the launch pad cup.
12. To launch, find an open area with no cars, pedestrians, or buildings within 50 feet. Make sure no one, including you, is in the flight path.
13. Stand to the side of the rocket while you're pumping it. Pump until the bottle flies into the air and stand back!

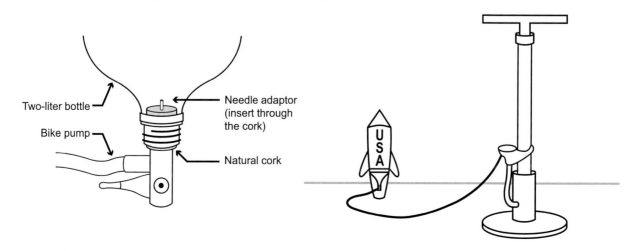

Two-liter bottle

Bike pump

Needle adaptor (insert through the cork)

Natural cork

Vendor and Store List

American Science & Surplus .... www.sciplus.com

Arbor Scientific .... www.arborsci.com

Blick Art Materials.. www.dickblick.com

Carolina Biological Supply .... www.carolina.com

Delta Education... www.deltaeducation.com

Demco .... www.demco.com

Educational Innovations .... www.teachersource.com

Edvotek: The Biotechnology Education Company .... www.edvotek.com

Fat Brain Toys .... www.fatbraintoys.com

Flinn Scientific.. www.flinnsci.com

Grainger Industrial Supply Company .... www.grainger.com

Lakeshore Learning... www.lakeshorelearning.com

Learning Resources.. www.learningresources.com

McMaster-Carr Supply Company .... www.mcmaster.com

Nasco.. www.enasco.com

Nature-Watch.. www.nature-watch.com

Pitsco Education... www.pitsco.com

S&S Worldwide .... www.ssww.com

STEM Supplies.. www.stem-supplies.com

Uline .... www.uline.com

Ward's Science.. www.wardsci.com

WebstaurantStore... www.webstaurantstore.com

Woodworks Ltd. .... www.craftparts.com

Program Planning Rubric

This is a worksheet to be used in developing a STEAM and Story program. Use this to help ensure you have all the components you wish to include in the program.

Program Name:

_____

Goals:
1. Books I will incorporate:
2. STEAM activities I will add:
3. Twenty-first-century skills employed in this program:
4. Social-emotional skills youths will practice:

Program outline:

_____

_____

Materials I will need:

_____

_____

Space setup needed:

_____

_____

Program promotion/building audience awareness:

_____

_____

Youth voice will be exercised by:

_____

_____

Ways we will reflect on what we have learned:

_____

_____

ABOUT THE AUTHORS

ELIZABETH McCHESNEY has over 30 years' experience in children's librarianship. In 2012, while serving as the Director of Children's Services for the Chicago Public Library, she led her team through the transformation of the summer reading program into the nationally recognized Summer Learning Challenge. This achievement earned her a *Library Journal* Movers & Shakers Award, the Founder's Award for Excellence from the National Summer Learning Association, and the John Cotton Dana Award. Liz believes in the role of STEAM-based library learning and finds great joy in watching children play, read, and learn in libraries. Liz writes and speaks extensively about library service to children, building successful partnerships, and the role of the twenty-first-century library. She passionately believes in the public library as a place of learning and education, joy and wonder for America's kids. Liz is now consulting on youth services and can be contacted at Liz@Lizmcc.net.

BRETT NICHOLAS is a former classroom teacher turned museum educator. He is a veteran developer of informal STEAM education programs for educators, students, families, and the public. For 15 years, Brett has worked at the Museum of Science and Industry and serves now as Manager of Community Initiatives, a role in which he is responsible for extending the reach of the museum's educational arm outside the walls of the museum. He's lectured and trained nationally and ardently believes in the role of STEAM in the library. Having set fire to balloons filled with explosive hydrogen gas, made fake poop to talk about digestion, and helped thousands of kids have their first dissection experience while cutting open cow eyeballs, Brett believes in direct and interactive teaching. He is dedicated to helping all children see how much fun they can have doing science and strives to open opportunities for science to have a meaningful role in their future. He currently serves as the Chief of Play and Learning at the DuPage Children's Museum.

INDEX